Instagram Marketing Mastery

Learn the Ultimate Secrets for Transforming Your Small Business or Personal Brand With the Power of Instagram Advertising for Beginners; Become a Famous Influencer

By Aaron Jackson

Table of Contents

Introduction

Congratulations on purchasing *Instagram Marketing Mastery* and thank you for doing so. The world is digitalizing quickly, with more and more technological tools and software emerging every day. The same has significantly impacted how businesses are conducted, especially when it comes to marketing. Digital marketing is one aspect that has become more rampant in the market today. Social media, mainly Instagram, has played a significant when it comes to the marketing of different products. Downloading this book is the first step in understanding how to master the art of marketing through Instagram and growing your business.

The following chapters will highlight some of the primary components of Instagram marketing before venturing into uploading your product for potential clients to view and purchase. That is, the book enables you to have a deeper understanding of what Instagram marketing is all about. Then, you will learn a step by step tutorial on how to successfully go into posting your product. With Instagram being an asset for Facebook, if you have once or twice sold on Facebook, then the process is quite similar. If not, then this book is what you have been looking for.

There are plenty of books on this subject on the market, thanks again for choosing this one! Every effort was made to ensure it is full of as much useful information as possible. Please enjoy!

Chapter 1: The Basics of Instagram and Why You Should Use It

In this chapter, you will learn about the basics of Instagram, from how you can create an account for the very advanced features. You will also find out why you should use Instagram to promote your product or market your business. Read on to find out!

What Is Instagram?

Instagram is a social media platform built for sharing videos and photos. It was first launched in October 2010 and was only available on iOS devices then. In April 2012, Instagram became available on Android devices. Facebook, which is owned by Mark Zuckerberg, purchased the service in 2012 and has since then held it.

Just like other social media platforms, Instagram gives you a chance to follow users you have interests in. It creates a news feed on the homepage displaying recent posts from the people you follow. You can comment on them or like them, depending on what you prefer.

Apart from posting videos and photos which stay on your profile permanently, Instagram created the latest addition in the form of Stories. Those of us that have used Snapchat before are familiar with this. Instagram stories allow you to share one or more photos and videos in a continuous series. Anyone can view the posts on Instagram stories within the next 24 hours, after which they automatically expire.

Instagram also supports direct messaging so you can be able to chat with people privately. You have the liberty to explore other people's profiles to find out which person you might be interested in.

How to Use Instagram

When you download Instagram, you will realize that the app has so many features, and for new users, it can be challenging to get started. I have outlined a beginner's guide that will guide you through the steps to becoming a pro on Instagram, from how you can create an account, to how you can find people and follow them.

How to Create an Instagram Account

To sign up for Instagram, you first need to get the mobile Instagram app by downloading it on an iOS (on App Store), Android phone (on Google Play Store), or Windows phones (Windows Phone Store). You can still use Instagram on computers through the Instagram URL.

Once you've downloaded the Instagram app, tap on its icon to open it. Select "Register with Email "to create an account using your email address, or you can sign up using your Facebook account by tapping on "Register with Facebook." If you chose to register with an email address, you would be prompted to create a username then come up with a password of your choice. After that, you will be required to fill out your profile information like your mobile number, among others. On the other hand, if you chose to create an account using Facebook, you will be prompted to sign in with your Facebook account, if you're still logged in (on Facebook), it will automatically create an account using your Facebook details.

After creating an account, the next thing you should do is editing your profile (if you feel it's necessary). You can edit your profile information like your name, your email address, or username by tapping the person icon in the toolbar section at the bottom of your screen. Tap on "Edit your Profile " and type the username you want, your website URL (if you have one), your brief bio, then tap "Save " if you're using an Android phone or "Done " if you're using an iPhone.

Navigating Instagram

After setting up your profile, it will show your bio and videos and photos you've ever posted on Instagram. You can be able to edit your profile info and adjust the account settings. To navigate to your profile, tap the person icon at the bottom screen and make the changes you wish by tapping on the "Edit Your Profile " button. You can access a lot more information and choices by tapping on the 'gear' icon. You can write a simple bio of up to 150 characters. You can also add or change the profile picture by importing photos from your phone's gallery, Twitter, or Facebook.

The camera allows you to take pictures using the Instagram camera or, instead, share photos from your phone's gallery. To access the camera, tap on the center icon from the toolbar at the bottom of the screen, you can take a photo or record a video, or choose a photo or video from your photo library.

To find people to follow, use the search and explorer function. You can access this function by tapping the magnifying glass icon from the toolbar at the bottom of the screen, toggle between the 'People' and 'Photos' views to explore posts and users, or you can type in the "Search" box and choose between 'Hashtags' and 'Users.'

The home page shows posts from you and other Instagram users you follow. As explained earlier, you can like (by tapping on the heart) or comment (by tapping on the comment icon and writing your comment) on the photos and videos in your news feed. You can access your news feed by tapping on the home button from the toolbar at the bottom of your screen.

The Activity tab shows the likes and comments on your photos and videos. You can access this tab by tapping on the speech bubble icon from the toolbar at the bottom of the screen and then toggle between the "Following "and "Your" views.

Finding Other Instagram Users to Follow

The Instagram app can help you find and follow people you might know. These are Facebook friends and people on your contact list that are using Instagram. To see these suggestions on an Android phone, go to your profile page and tap on the icon with three vertical dots on your top right side of the screen. Tap on 'Find Friends' and then select find friends from Facebook, from your phone's contact list or Instagram, suggested users. Tap on "follow" next to the users whose posts you will like to see appear in your feed.

If you're using an iOS app, navigate to your profile and tap on the gear in the top right corner of your screen. Choose the "Find People to Follow" icon and select whether to find friends from Facebook, from your phone's contact list, or from Instagram suggested users. Tap the "follow" icon next to users you would like to see their posts in your feed. To find people to follow on a Windows Phone Instagram app, go to your profile and tap on the icon with three horizontal dots at the bottom right corner of your screen. Tap on Settings, then choose "Find and Invite Friends." After that, tap "Find your friends" to find friends from either Facebook or your contact list. To find friends from Instagram, tap on "Suggested Users" and tap on "follow" next on those whose posts you'd like to be appearing in your feed.

How to Post a Photo On Instagram

When posting a photo on Instagram, you have two options, taking one with the Instagram camera or uploading one from the phone gallery. To do this, tap on the camera icon at the bottom center of your screen. From your camera, you can switch the photo grid on and off, switch between a selfie or back camera, or choose whether to use the flash or not. To take a photo, tap the shutter button or hit the video icon to record a video. Instagram allows you to add effects from the editing tools at the top of your screen or use filters instead. You can add a caption to your photo, tag people in it, add your location, or share it with other social media platforms like Twitter, Facebook, Tumblr, or Flickr. When adding a caption, you can use #hashtags and @mentions. Mentioning enables you to alert another user of your post; they will get a notification that you mentioned them. Hashtags, on the other hand, will help other Instagram users (even those that don't follow you) find your posts.

Adding to Your Instagram Story

To create new content for your Instagram story, slide to the left. This will open a new panel with a wide range of options: Boomerang (a short looping video), music to add some flavor to your story and

Type to post a text instead. You will also see the Live option that broadcasts live from your phone to your followers.

To share a photo on your Instagram story, click on the camera icon, take a photo using the Instagram camera, or choose one from your phone library. You can edit it before sharing by using the Instagram editing tool then post it by clicking on 'Share.' You can follow the same process when sharing a video.

Why Should You Use Instagram?

You might wonder what's the purpose of using Instagram when there are so many other social media platforms. Well, Instagram's main draw is that it is based around photos that are very easy to take using a smartphone. You don't need to carry an actual camera to share what is happening around you, just snap a pic, apply a few filters, and you're good to go. Instagram isn't just a concern for ordinary people; it can be used as an advertising tool for businesses and products.

Why Use Instagram for Your Business?

Your business isn't on Instagram? You're missing out! Let me give you reasons as to why you should consider adding your business on Instagram.

Since its inception in 2010, Instagram has proved to be a potent marketing tool. Below are some of the reasons Instagram can benefit your business.

Many People Are Using Instagram

According to recent statistics, there are over 1 billion active users on Instagram. With these numbers, there are no limits to the success of a business if a dedicated Instagram strategy is applied.

Any Business Can Thrive Regardless of the Size

With the high number of users to choose from, a business can achieve so much. This applies to both the large, well-established companies as well as the small companies or one-person operations. Even for the well-established companies, success doesn't come overnight, but it takes a spirited effort like keeping an active online presence and maintaining a consistent routine of sharing at least one post a day. This is precisely how household franchises like Nike and Pepsi have effectively used Instagram to grow.

You Can Make Money Directly From Instagram

Having evolved through the years, Instagram now has a greater emphasis on generating revenue through product placement. The latest platform you can do this from is the Shoppable Posts: it allows businesses to add tags to their photos with links that include price and ability to "shop now" and product description of which leads the user to the online store. With this feature, it is effortless for businesses to attract actual sales from Instagram. A study shows that as of 2019, seventy-two percent of Instagram users have purchased products using the platform.

Instagram Stories Make Your Business Relatable

Instagram provides various ways you can share information about your business, but the best way you can do so is through the use of live stories. You can share insights into your business and how you come up with your products or services. This can be done through sharing interesting videos of how your products are made and live Q % A sessions between you and your audience. Live posts are an excellent way to build trust, rapport, and credibility with your followers. If consumers see your business isn't just about making money, they will trust your brand more.

You Can Partner With Influencers

For those who might not know, influencers are online celebrities who can promote a brand and push it into the mainstream.

A good influencer increases your business's sales through increased return on investment and access to people you wouldn't usually reach. They can spread the word of your business to millions of followers within a few posts.

Chapter 2: The Power of Instagram Advertising for Beginners in Business and Personal Brand Transformation

Instagram came into public realization around 2010, and like any other social media, it created a platform where people can share ideas, their likes and dislikes, suggestions, and any other debatable politics. However, it came with a unique strategy of using, majorly, images. It started as a simple image sharing application, but now it has developed into a complete channel that can be used in marketing.

For a promised success in your venture, you must invest in a marketing docket. Otherwise, you may end up having dead stocks and retardations in the growth of your company. Marketing can be enhanced by reaching potential clients and explain to them why your product suits them. Instagram, as a social media platform, can be used to reach more potential and enhance the services to regular clients.

Lately, Instagram has released more tools to enhance the growth of any business. Such features include those of analytics, a new way to drive traffic from Instagram stories, clickable posts, video platforms, and IGTV.

Reasons as to Why You Should Use Instagram Marketing for The Success of Your Business

The human mind is designed in a way that associates particular imagery to a given characteristic. However, this depends on the stored knowledge of a person. That notwithstanding, a person feels freer and safer to purchase a commodity he or she knows about. As a result, image and video sharing have been established to most effective, especially when advertising a new commodity or reaching a new market.

Instagram has overtaken other social media platforms in image and video sharing. This makes it more suitable for running advertisements and reaching clients. It has been established that most of the Instagram users are more than merely engaged as they are commonly online shoppers. Consequently, many buyers have ended up settling on certain decisions after seeing a product on Instagram.

The mentioned fact makes the Instagram users the best audience and, with enhanced convincing and implementation of the tips to be mentioned, you may win more clients than before.

Another reason why Instagram is a recommendable tool to reach more clients and the market at larger is that they understand business. Instagram has developed features that favor e-commerce and the overall operation of a business, particularly the marketing docket.

Steps of Success through Instagram Ecommerce Platform

Once you have resorted to making better use of this platform, then you must apply particular strategies to reach potential clients. Similarly, Instagram will not help you reach a large number and but also a number that can convince the unbelieving that you are the best. Remember, numbers do not lie. Below are the steps you should follow in order to successfully drive your business to greatness and increase your competence by reaching many consumers of your products or services.

Set your Objective and Goal: What do you wish to achieve by employing Instagram e commerce? With established goals and objectives, it easy to formulate your strategies and approaches. The goals can or maybe a given target of clients you wish to have reached annually. Similarly, it can be a target of reaching a particular group of people in large numbers or maybe a target sale per unit time.

Identify Your Target Clients: First, you should know what kind of client you would wish to reach, of course, in regard to your services. Identifying your target clients will help you in the allocation of resources in a more economical way. After identifying the target potential, you can choose now the target audience from where you can get potential clients. After identifying the target audience, take your time to understand their culture. By understanding your clients, you will be able to customize your advertisement, products, and services that you offer.

Audit your Instagram Account: If you have been a user of the platform, go through it and see the activities that you have been doing. Each aspect of your account should match the intention of the business; these aspects include profile, hashtags, feeds, bio, and also the captions. Similarly, the account you follow should be in line with your business. The audit should be based on the goals of your business, the target clients, and the target audience.

Set a Business Profile for your Instagram Account: Truly, Instagram has embraced the business owner and gave them a warm welcome by establishing features that are solely meant for business activities. Instagram has sought to enhance the activities of the business. As a result, they have established a business profile that enables the user to add links in the stories, create clickable posts, and auto-publishing to Instagram. Below are the steps by step of setting an Instagram business profile.

1. Create a business Facebook page. Firstly, open a Facebook application and click on the 'create page' from the options given in the dropdown menu. Secondly, choose your business type in the 'category' option and name your page. Remember, it is a business account; therefore, formality should be followed. The name given should be a keyword that a person can search when in need to reach your business. Thirdly, upload a profile and cover photo that portrays your business. This can be your business logo or the product/service you offer. Fourthly, add the description and links that direct the page visitors to do an action like visiting your website or other platforms that have more information. The description should give the visitor an insight into who you are and what you deal with the shortest words possible. Finally, make sure that everything is in order as per your wish.

2. Link your Business Facebook page to your Instagram account. Firstly, log in to your Instagram account and click on your profile. Secondly, tap the 'gear' icon in the top right of the screen to open the account setting. Thirdly, click 'Switch to Business Profile' and then 'Continue' to link the Instagram account to your Facebook account. Fourthly, ensure the profile is set to be viewed by the public; otherwise, your business profile will not be validated. Fifthly, click 'Continue As' to connect to Facebook, and when your Facebook page appears to tap 'Next.' If your Facebook page does not appear, it means you are not listed as an admin of the page, and you can change the setting via the Facebook application.

3. Set your Instagram Business Profile. After the above steps, you will be prompted to add your address, that is, phone number, email, physical addresses. The entered information is vital as it is the one used by your willing-to-buy followers.

Formulate a Precise, Comprehensive, and an Appealing Bio: Your bio should inform your audience who you are and why they should follow you. It can be hard to formulate one, but with set goals and know-about of your target audience, it is easy. To make your bio appealing and attractive to many of your audience, you should include the following:

o Your actual name or your business's name. Most of the followers will search you by the title of your name or the business. Depending on the one that has more weight, between the business and personal name, include one or both to guarantee your visitors that it is the real you.

o Your Instagram username and optimize the use of '@' and '#' signs. Use of the tags before a description creates a link that will lead the visitor to either a feed in your site or externally to your website or blogs. Similarly, use the keywords that can be used to search your business.

- o Links to your website or blog. Share a link that directs your visitors to your website homepage or blog. Alternatively, it can direct them to a particular product or information as per your objective.
- o Your contact information. Insert information about how potential clients can reach you. Provide your contact number, physical address, and email among any other channel your clients can reach you through.
- o You may also include any other information about your skills, preferences, achievements, and other characteristics that can trigger 'friendship' with your clients.

Enhance your Instagram Business Profile: Since you have now set a business profile, you are few steps towards creating your success. However, make sure that your profile conveys the message you wish the visitors and followers to know about your business. Some of the users will just scan through your account, and if not satisfied by the profile or the feeds, the chances are that you have lost them. Therefore, your feeds should comprehensively convey the message and at the same time, be visually appealing.

Sell your Brand through the Instagram Stories: Remember your objectives and overall goal that you wish to achieve and customize the particulate message you wish to pass to your potential followers and clients. Instagram stories can be compared to the movie trailer; they tell your audience followers what to expect from you. Do not generalize your stories; instead, categorize them in a way that your audience can comprehend the content in regard to their preferences.

Audit Your Account Again: Now that you have set an Instagram business profile, revisit the account as a visitor. Identify any gap or inconsistency in your communication and the information provided.

Strategizing Instagram Content

Strategy, in this case, means that you will not post anyhow; you have to manage the account with keenness and formality. Your feeds should not be in any way politically inclined. You are dealing with different people who have different perceptions and societal norms.

Therefore, maintain decency and orderly and neutralism in all your feeds. After all, you are there to convert people to be your clients, and your business is to convince them why your product or services suits them, period. Since Instagram allows only four types of the post, below are the considerations you should take on each.

Video Posts

You should always make a video that is informant, precise, and not lengthy. Similarly, the video should be clear, and the associated sound is audible.

How to Use Video Post to Boost your Business

Video posts are common in Instagram feeds; however, if you want the best from it, you have to strategize what and how to do it.

Features of a Good Video Post

Run a promotion of your products: Since video posts can convey a lot of information in a short time, you should utilize them to sell your product and services. A single image cannot display or showcase much information compared to a 1-minute video. Similarly, a video post allows the followers to see the product in more than one dimension, unlike in a photo. Therefore, make sure you capture only the relevant information that will give a potential customer comprehensive information.

Associate it with your Brand: A video post that introduces your company or brand can be the best tool for advertising your brand. Create a video that associates the product to your particular brand. Eventually, your followers will have trust with the brand and, in turn, your business.

Educate your Audience on how to Efficiently use your Product or Services: Through your video posts, share a short tutorial about your product and how transforming, effective, or useful it is. This will be a form of advertisement and, at the same time, a lesson for your followers. The interested followers will be more interested after watching a video that enlightens them. Similarly, you will give an insight into how and about your product to followers who could not have met such a product or service.

Photo Posts

Ensure that your photos are clear and compatible. You have the option to post the photo in either landscape, square, or portrait formats. Therefore, choose the format that gives a quality impression.

Shopping Posts

Shopping posts allows the follower to click the post and view the information about the product. Additionally, they are directed to a URL where they can purchase the products. Therefore, make sure your URL is valid, and the 'about' of the commodity or services matches the actual one.

Carousel Posts

This is a new feature that many businesses have embraced to promote their new products. The feature allows you to share a photo alongside a video. Therefore, make sure the content of the photo and the video do rhyme; otherwise, you will create ambiguity in your communication.

How to Enhance and Boost Your Business Using Carousel Posts

Use Carousel Posts When launching a new Product: You can share multiple photos to give your followers an insight into how the new product is. However, incorporation of a video alongside the photos will enhance the comprehension of your followers. When the potential customer gets a clear insight into your product and, in some ways, it fits his or her preferences, you have actually 'enticed' him or her to try your products and services.

It is the best in Sharing Insights of an Event: Your business or organization may be having an event that is so vital to your business. Traditionally, you can upload thousands of photos to make your followers 'taste the feeling'. However, the high chances are that some of your followers will not be able to go through all the photos and will have incomplete news. Instead, use Carousel Posts to share the event since it is brief but informative.

Use Carousel Post to Show What-Can-Do of your Product: Among your followers, there happens to be some or many, depending on the commodity, who are not aware of what your product or service can do. As a result, a Carousel post can be the best to share the before-scenario and after-scenario. Through a Carousel post, your followers will be able to deduce the meaning and effectiveness of your product or service.

How to Make Use of Instagram Stories to Boost your Business

Instagram stories is an essential marketing strategy. In fact, many businesses create more stories to capture new and potential clients.

Share the Story Regularly: Any ordinary story on Instagram lasts for 24 hours; therefore, to reach the maximum number of potential clients, you should post stories regularly, making sure each of the moment the followers have something to munch on their mind.

You can Share Anytime at your Convenience: For regular Instagram posts, you have to time when most of your target followers are active. However, since the content will be available for 24 hours, if the follower will be active within 24 hours, he or she can view the content. Similarly, you can share the status as a highlight. It will last even much longer.

Make your Story more appealing by incorporating fun, information, and promotional content: Remember, you should fully engage your followers for them to read and view your feeds. Therefore, do not be so serious until you intimidate them or make them feel not welcomed. On the other hand, do not be very jokey until your followers do not recognize when you mean business. Balance all the aspects. Make your posts informative for your followers to learn more, funny to put across even the sensitive message, and promotional content to remind your followers who you are and what you offer.

Chapter 3: Tips About Posting on Instagram to Get the Best Results

Instagram is a social networking platform that allows people to share photos and videos. Mike Krieger and Kevin Systrom founded Instagram and saw its launching in October 2010. The application is owned by Facebook and allows use on Android and Windows devices. Users can upload photos or videos to the application, edit them with some filters, and easily organize them following their location information as well as tags. One can share their uploads publicly or with their private followers only. Other users can browse through the service and view the trending information and content. They can like videos and photos as well as follow other users so that they can add a feed to their content.

Initially, Instagram only allowed its users to frame their content in a square. However, in 2015, the restrictions were eliminated, and other features were added to the application. These features were, for instance, the ability to upload several videos or pictures on a single post, messaging features, and adding stories to an upload. Despite other social media platforms, Instagram has gained its popularity quite rapidly. By May 2019, the application had over one billion registered users. By October 2015, Instagram had over 40 billion photos uploaded.

Instagram, as an Android app, has gone through some major updates. The first update was introduced in 2014 March, whereby the size of the application was cut by half. Some significant improvements were made to improve the performance of the app on Android devices. The main reason behind this improvement was because half of the Instagram users owned Android devices and were outside the United States. In April 2017, the second update was made. The offline mode feature was added. This meant that the content that was initially loaded on the application's news feed could be available even with no internet connection. Users were also given the ability to like, comment, save photos and videos, as well as following and unfollowing users, which could be affected once they connect to the internet.

The initial founders of Instagram, Systrom, and Krieger stepped down from Instagram in 2018 September, and Adam Mosseri took the position to head Instagram. Another feature was added to Instagram in November 2018, whereby visually impaired people could listen to explanations on each photo through the alternative text. The text is either generated automatically or a text inputted by the user.

Photographic Filters

Some photographic filters are offered by Instagram to enable users to edit their photos. These include:

Normal- This means that there are no filters applied

1977- This means a red tint in increased exposure fiving the image a brighter and faded look.

Brannan- This feature adds to the contrast, exposure, and increases metallic tint.

Hudson-The The feature creates an illusion that is icy, increasing the shadows, dodged center, and cool tint.

Valencia- The image becomes quite faded, the exposure is increased, and some warming colors are added to make the feeling quite antique.

Video

In June 2013, Instagram allowed users to share 15-second videos on their timelines. This feature permitted Instagram to remain competitive with other social media networks. By the end of 2015, Instagram had added some elements that could support windscreen videos. The limitation on 15 seconds video was updated in 2016, whereby users could upload a 60 seconds video. At the beginning of 2017, there was an introduction of Albums, which allowed users to upload videos taking ten minutes on a single post.

IGTV

Instagram launched the feature in June 2018. It can be described as a vertical video app that can function both on Instagram's website as well as the application itself. The primary function of IGTV is to allow registered users to upload 10-minute videos with a limit size of 650MBs. Users that are verified on Instagram can post videos taking 60 minutes with a magnitude of 5.4 GB.

Instagram Direct

Instagram Direct was launched in December 2013. The feature allows users to communicate via private messaging. This means that users that follow each other can interact through messages which they can as well send pictures and videos. In a case where one user is not followed by the other, and they send a message, it is usually marked as awaiting, and they must accept to open the message. An Instagram user can post a message or photo to 15 people at maximum. Consistent updates on the application allowed the users to directly reply to private messages by the use of emoji, text, or a click on the heart icon. There is a camera icon in the Direct where users can take videos or photos without having to leave the conversation. It is also possible to send website links using the Direct as well as posting pictures without having to crop them.

User Characteristics

Demographics. Registered Instagram users are equally divided. This means that 50% of users own iPhones, and the other 50% use Android devices. The number of females using Instagram is quite higher than that of the male. 68% of females use the application, and only 32% of users are male. The number of users living in urban areas is also higher than that of users residing in suburban and rural areas. The number of young people that is below 35years of age is higher than that of older people. This is because young people are more attracted to the application. Educated people prove to be the most active users of Instagram and followed by high school graduates.

User engagement. The content shared on Instagram timeline dramatically determines how the users are engaged. When faces are revealed, many people are likely to comment and like the photos or videos uploaded. When fewer individuals are depicted on upload, the more the number of users are engaged. To enhance user engagement, Instagram has come up with a feature that allows users to apply for verification on their account badge. However, not everyone who applies for the verification gets a blue tick.

Trends- Instagram users can create trends using hashtags. The hashtag involves particular keywords with a hash symbol combined. The hashtags allow users to share information with other users easily. It is one of the most popular trends on social media. It is used by highlighting a particular day or time and choosing the material to post on. A feature named "follow" was added on the hashtag whereby on pressing it, users can see highlights of some content on their feeds.

Motives among young adults. Looking at posts, interacting as well as passing time are some of the motives a significant number of young people use Instagram. This is because young people prefer visual communication to any other form of communication.

Features that Distinguish Instagram from other Social Media Applications

In the modern world, multiple social media applications are available to us. These platforms give us an opening to share photos, videos, and ideas to those following us. Every social media platform has its uniqueness, meaning that each has its aspects that are different from the other. However, the best platform available to almost everyone in the Instagram app. It has its superiority above other platforms because it has multiple features that are not available in other applications. Typically, it has a combination of features from all most every social media platform. It can be described as an all-inclusive application. As said earlier, it allows users to post their pictures, videos, and use captions on their uploads. Tagging other users is also possible when one uploads a photo or video. Direct messaging is also enhanced by the app, where people can privately text their colleagues, family, and friends.

Using Instagram helps people to avoid clustering their phones with many social media applications. The "My Story" feature, for instance, allows users to upload pictures and videos on their story and makes it visible to everyone. Other users can like, comment, or reply to the uploads much easily. Pictures being uploaded can be edited using the filter features provided, locations tagged, friends, and writing an unlimited word caption. This is, unlike other platforms, whereby the word count is limited.

Instagram allows users to privatize their accounts. This way, only the people one accepts to follow can view their uploads. When one finds out that another user is acting maliciously on their account, they can report them. The accounts of such people are deemed to be inappropriate.

On a business note, Instagram is also considered one of the best platform for marketing on social media. Social media marketing has widely grown, replacing traditional marketing methods. This is because most people spend their time on social media, thus making it a great platform to market products and services. Instagram has proved to be the best in marketing because of the following three factors.

Better Target Market Penetration: young adults tend to be impulse buyers, thus influencing their shopping choices on Instagram is quite more effortless. A wide range of Instagram users are below the age of 35 years and own an Instagram account. An experienced business person will easily convince the youths to buy his products and services by assuring them of their effectiveness. Most of these youths are making a lot of money, and therefore buying will not be a problem as long as the product is well represented. Instagram is an outstanding application because users' business people can upload videos of the product may be demonstrating its use and the variety that is available. A video can also be uploaded on the services one offers, thus attracting a more extensive customer base. Females take the most significant portion of Instagram users, and it is evident that they love shopping; therefore, Instagram proves to be the best platform.

Better display of content. As an entrepreneur displaying products or services, Instagram allows for incredible customer engagement. Instagram allows for User Interface, thus making one create advance their brand by uploading pictures and videos in a much effective way. Images or videos uploaded are well displayed, thus minimizing cluttering that could probably put off potential customers.

Instagram users are most active and spend much of their time on the platform. This is one of the features that makes Instagram outshine other platforms in social media. Past studies reveal that a considerable number of users are more likely to like, reply or comment, and even share images uploaded on Instagram, unlike in other platforms. When a business picture or video is shared or commented on multiple times, it reaches a broader population, which is the best thing that could happen to your business. The customer base for a particular activity is likely to widen.

Tips About Posting on Instagram to Get the Best Results

To increase the engagement one has on Instagram, it is crucial to what they post, how they post when to post, and how often they should post. Everyone on the platform hopes to increase the number of likes and ensure more people are engaged in what they post. In many cases, users will make simple things complicated, thus failing to achieve whatever they want. The following are some tips Instagram users can consider to increase the number of followers, likes, comments, and shares on the uploads they make.

Sharing high-quality photos and videos. This is one of the simplest things people can do when uploading pictures and videos, but they often complicate it. It can be done by ensuring the photographs or videos being uploaded are not pixilated, blurred, or dark. The focus of the user should be mainly on the quality of the video or photo being uploaded. It should be quite simple, whereby it is not cluttered or multiple fonts used and squeezed in a single upload. Getting more likes entirely depends on how well the photos or videos are displayed. An explicit video will always get a user many views as well as downloads and is shared widely.

Writing some engaging and exciting captions. Simply uploading an image is not enough; the caption that follows the image plays a significant role in determining the number of users you engage in. The caption should be value-packed and interesting to attract multiple followers and other users. Single-word and one-word sentences should be eliminated. An Instagram user should focus on telling details that are quite evoking and inspiring. The audience will always be attracted to a post that has a relatable caption that is humorous or inspiring and will most definitely follow back, like, and comment on the uploaded picture or video. It is essential to work on several captions on different posts and see which gets more likes and comments and try to perfect its user to increase the coverage.

Using a call to action. To achieve what you want, you must communicate to your audience effectively. You can easily include a call to your audience to like, comment, or share your upload. The request you try to engage your audience in should be polite and relatable to the post you have made. For instance, if your post was about an experience you had in high school, you can end your caption like "like and comment below if you had the same experiences in high school." Using a different call to action statements is vital as it helps to engage more users. For instance, if it's a video, "link on my bio, comment, tag your friends and share" statement can be used. This way, people will always find themselves replying and liking your uploads, thus giving you a multitude of followers and likes on Instagram.

Knowing who your audience is. You must be comfortable with the audience you are targeting in your uploads. You should know what your target audience likes, maybe memes, travel photos, or food pictures. Creating content that is appealing to your audience will increase the number of likes you get on the uploads you make.

Considering Instagram is quite easy to use, you can observe keenly what your target audience finds pleasant and always deliver to them a variety of what they want. Your number of followers will also increase as many people will want to know more about what you are posting on your Instagram page.

Always remember to add a Geolocation to each post you make. The geolocation is a simple location text that usually appears above an upload. The number of likes this small text can gain you is quite significant. It is essential always to consider what locations your audience finds interesting. Using those locations as the short text above, your uploads will always reach multiple people. Instagram users need to make sure that they add the location at the time they upload a picture or video.

Consistently like, comment, and share each day. To gain more likes on Instagram, you have to give yours to other people. To add to the number of people engaged in your posts, it is essential to consider engaging with fellow Instagram users. Showing genuine interest on other users' uploads shows some support for them and encourages them to check on your timeline. This way, they will most likely like and comment on uploads you have made on your page, thus adding to your feed.

Using the right hashtags. The right hashtags will always make it easier for a user to gain more likes and followers. This is because they help in widely engaging Instagram users and allow you to be ahead of competitors. In every single post made, a user should consider using varied hashtags in describing the target audience or the account. An Instagram user should try to make their hashtags as unique as possible to attract more followers. Commonly used hashtags will always put off potential followers and likes because people are already too used to them.

Encouraging people to tag a friend or follower. This is one of the best techniques you can use in the bid to increase your number of followers, likes, and comments. One should call on their audience to tag a friend or famous follower on the post made. An Instagrammer should ensure their post is engaging and interesting for other people to find value in tagging friends or sharing the post. For instance, if it is in the case of a ladies' jeans business, you can add a call on followers to tag along with ladies who should accompany them to the particular ladies' jeans shop. This way, the post is even likely to get shared more, thus increasing the number of likes to your feed. The number of followers will also double as people will desire to know more about the business you are working on.

Consistently using Instagram stories. Active users on Instagram stories are about ten million all over the world. This means that Instagram stories should not be ignored. This can be done by uploading stories on the Instagram page and calling on people to check or watch it out. Likes and traffic on posts made are likely to be boosted a great deal.

Hosting giveaways. This is one of the things that the audience on Instagram finds attractive and follow back the accounts that are hosting the giveaways. This can be done by inciting the audience on a note that qualifying for the giveaways requires them to like, comment, and share a particular post. An interested audience will do as instructed so that they can be eligible. Adding some qualifications, such as telling them to tag friends, also works best when one wants to increase the number of followers on their feeds. It can as well help in reaching out to a broader audience. When a user wins the giveaways being hosted, it becomes a win for both parties. In many cases, others will follow back on the account so that they may stand a chance to win given another opportunity.

Always consider tagging accounts that are relevant to the post made. When relevant or popular people are tagged along in a post, a wider audience is reached. This is because whenever they are ta, a notification will always pop on their feeds, and it will be visible to their audience. Their attention will be grabbed and will be interested in following the particular account.one should always ensure that the people they are tagging on their brand are relevant to it to avoid it being saved as spam.

Posting on a regular schedule is another technique to increase followers, likes, shares, and comments. To achieve the best results, one should set up a schedule when to post. This will help in ensuring that the audience is always engaged. One can try to identify the time many users are online and post at that particular time. This way, a post is likely to get more likes and shares.

Chapter 4: Creating Stories and Engaging with Your Audience through Instagram

Instagram is simply a social networking platform where you can share videos and photos. It was officially launched in October of 2019 on iOS. In April of 2012, it became available on Android, and at the same time, Facebook purchased it and has since been under its ownership.

Advantages of using Instagram

- Instagram is mainly based around photos that are currently very easy to take using smartphones. You can share your world with others through a simple snapshot.

- You can be simply a lurker – this means you can be a follower without posting anything. It is acceptable to just be a follower of your friends, fans, and celebrities if that is what brings joy to you.

- It's an effective tool for advertising. You can promote your blogs or sell products on Instagram.

Basics Of Creating A Story On Instagram

First, you open Instagram then tap on the camera icon at the upper left- corner on your phone.

Share a video or photo that you have already captured by swiping on your screen and browsing on the gallery or choose on camera to capture a photo or video in the app.

There are options you can choose from;

Live

A live option gives you an option of immediate filming and broadcasting live. Friends can follow leaving comments, and when you finish broadcasting, you can either allow the video to disappear, save or share for the next 24 hours.

Normal

When you tap, it captures a photo, and when you hold down, it records a video. Instagram stories are normally 15 seconds long, in case your story is longer use 'CutStory' to split it to 15 seconds installments.

Boomerang

Boomerang mode films allow looping GIFs of up to three seconds in length.

Superzoom

Superzoom is a video recording lens that can zoom closer on your subject at the same time, turn up the volume. It can create a dramatic soundtrack accompanying your video

Rewind

Here you use the rewind lens to film in reverse a video.

Stop Motion

This lens films cool stop-motion videos. These are several still images woven together to one seamless video.

Hands-Free

Here you simply use hands-free mode to set up a camera to film a video.

After editing your photo or video, you tap on 'your story' or 'next' to share. You can save your edited video or photo in your gallery by tapping 'Save.'

How to Engage the Audience on Instagram

· Making use of influencers

Reach out to influential Instagram accounts and users. Social media influencers are considered modern-day celebrities. Having a collaboration with influencer's shows, you are well informed about recent trends.

Partner with influencers that have not only big following but the right following that you can engage with. This is the kind of following that you are able to be part of their conversation. This is much easier than starting your own from scratch.

· Use Regramming

Regramming is posting a photo that is from someone else account to your own. This is one of the most effective and easiest ways to engage the audience. It creates a mutually beneficial relationship turning a casual fan into an ambassador.

Your feed is also to fill up with great photos saving you the time of shooting the photos yourself. Your regrammed photos will most likely prompt more fans to share more creating a cycle of User Generated Content (UGC)

Tips of attracting UGC on Instagram include;

Use of compelling hashtag

Organizing photo contest through Instagram

Being on top of your tagged images

Encouraging photo submissions

Using your captions to prompt discussions

Remember, Instagram is a visual social network, and photos matter most; hence, can be used to prompt further engagement. Spend ample time crafting a captivating caption that brings life to your image prompting followers to relate to your content.

Have a consistent voice such as soft guidelines, fitting lyrics, adding timestamps or date, and the like that encourage followers to respond.

· Be part of the comment threads

Monitor the comments, either positive or negative. Appreciate followers for kind comments or for tagging their friends. Respond to comments that enquire more about the photo.

Being responsive to comments proves to your followers that you care, and they are important to you. It also builds loyalty.

· Be involved in contest and campaigns

Instagram has the option of running contests that can help build a following and also increase engagement. Some of these contests to consider include;

Like contests – Here, you simply request users to like your photo to be able to enter a contest and win a prize.

Comment Contests – Here, they enter the contest by commenting on your photo. There can, for example, be asked to tag three friends or tell why they want to win the prize. This type of contest allows you to receive relevant feedback and also direct traffic to your account.

Regram contest – Here, you request those that want to enter the contest to regram an image is tagging your account. This way, you get the benefit of not only your followers but even the followers of your followers.

Photo Challenge contest – This is a popular Instagram contest using hashtags.

Figuring Out Ideas On An Instagram Story

Instagram story feature is one of the most popular components. It a powerful platform that boosts engagement in the app. below we look at some story ideas that boost effective engagement;

· Go Live

Anything can happen at a live feed, and many users are likely to tune in. Also, in live feed questions are attended to quickly, making it a perfect place for quick question and answers session. Before the Live Instagram, your followers will receive notification of your intended live streaming, helping to build your live audience.

After the live streaming, you can upload it to your stories, making it possible for your followers who could not tune in to have an opportunity to view it later.

· Driving users to your content

You can use a compelling call to action on your story hence driving traffic to your site. Note that Instagram allows a 'swipe up link' to be added to your story. For example, Starbucks was promoting its new cold-brewed beverages on their Instagram stories. They invited followers to swipe up to place their orders.

Other additional uses or the link feature include;

To announce blog content

Promote lengthy content like tutorial and webinars

Tease exclusive content

· Offer a sneak peek

You can use Instagram stories to tease a coming event or upcoming announcement to your Instagram followers, making them feel special. These make them plan to come for the real event. Such gestures help build trust and gives your followers a great reason to follow your account.

· Have a behind the scene for followers

You can have a behind-the-scene element like a popular recipe story or a day in the life of an employee, just to build a deeper and more intimate connection with followers. It adds a 'human' element in the Instagram stories.

· Poll your audience

This is a new feature on Instagram. It's a really fun way to engage followers. For example, sports teams have used polls on Instagram for fans to predict the outcome of a game.

It's simple to create a poll on Instagram. You just record your story, then open the stickers menu and tap on the poll sticker. Here you will be requested to add a question ad customize your choice of answers. Followers will now be able to cast their vote and view the results anytime they come back to view the Story.

Apps That Enhance Instagram Stories

There are many Instagram Story editor apps available in the market that are capable of improving your Instagram experience. Below we look at a few of this;

· Adobe Spark Post

Adobe Spark Post offers animated effects for a photo. It supports iOS, Android, and desktop platforms. It comes packaged with sizing options for any size of content fed. Most people prefer converting their photos to four seconds of video for sharing as stories on Instagram.

To use the app, tap the green + sign at the bottom of the screen. Select the background image, either a solid color or photo. When the story is ready, share it by simply tapping the button. You can also save stories on your camera.

· Videoshop

It's available on both Android and iOS.

To add new content to the app, tap the + icon at the top right corner. To add more clips, locate the + icon at the bottom. The advantage of Videoshop is you can automatically open the size of the clip import. If the imported clip is not in a position, you can swipe to several options beneath the clip then select options for the setting.

· Filmmaker Pro

This iOS app allows you to edit square (1:1) clip, landscape (16:9 and portrait (9:16) video clips with ease. To switch to the app, tap the + sign. To switch to color modes, tap the gear icon on the left. Its standout feature is that you can install custom fonts. Meaning you can email a font file to self then tap to open it from your mobile. Thereafter the font will be available automatically whenever you wish.

· Hype Type

This iOS app allows the addition of animated custom text on over boomerangs and video clips. You may not be able to customize colors and fonts, but its intuitive interface is beautiful. It supports music overlays on recorded video clips and can trim clips to various desired dimensions.

While using this app, keep video clips between five and fifteen seconds long. Also, using this app, you can create cool graphics to use in Instagram Story and blog posts when desired.

· Font Candy

Font Candy has gained its adoration and popularity in the recent past. It's an iOS app because it's simple to operate. Font Candy app comes with cool artworks and interesting, fun fonts to play with when adding your photos.

Checking Into The Analytics

· Increasing the engagement rate

You can increase the engagement rate by comparing Instagram post to know the most engaging content by;

Calculating the engagement rate

Ranking post by their engagement rate

Noting the best performing post

· Optimizing your posting times

Optimize your posts by getting more likes, comments, and views on your content by;

Calculating the top seven best posting time that gets the most engagement

Discovering when your audience is most active

Using location data to point out top time zones

· Attracting the right followers

Attract the right followers by knowing who are getting attracted by your account through;

Using demographic data like gender and age to guide you on content strategy

Find out the location of your followers by city, country, and language spoken

Track your follower's growth rate and view their profile regularly

By using Instagram Hashtag Analytics, you will know which hashtags are performing best

Using Stories As Part Of A Business In Instagram

Instagram stories are an easy and quick way to engage with other followers and users. A study conducted by Microsoft reveals average human attention had dropped from twelve to eight seconds in 2017. It is mainly due to the proliferation of technology.

Instagram stories somehow cater to this kind of generation where people have a shorter attention span. This is because, through Instagram stories, you can only post videos that are 15 seconds long per time.

Another thing is that this feature is available for mobile. Therefore, it can be posted anytime and anywhere, making it accessible. These stories do disappear after every 24 hours, so there is no need to worry if it doesn't fit your feed.

Businesses should take advantage of Instagram stories because of the following benefits:

- Through Instagram, they can post as much content as desired
- Instagram will help the business to grow an audience
- Instagram will allow the business to engage regularly with their audience by setting up polls, asking questions and allowing followers to ask questions and tagging other people
- Instagram will help to drive traffic to websites

In Summary

Instagram has greatly grown over the years and continues to broaden its horizons. It's appealing to all kinds of people from vacationers, advertisers, influencers, brands, and many more.

It has proved to be a powerful marketing tool for small and big businesses looking forward to increasing their reach and visibility.

Chapter 5: Secrets to Help You Grow Your Profile and Your Audience on Instagram

One of the strategies of growing your small business is applying social networking sites (SNS). These sites help you to connect with various people, not only at the local but also on the global stage. Unlike the traditional media that do not allow two-way communication, the social networking sites let you understand the feedback from the audience about the information that you have shared. The response you get from your audience assists in reinforcing the message or improve it. There are various types of social media sites. Examples of such sites include Facebook, WhatsApp, Twitter, Snapchat, Flickr, and Instagram. Some sites allow a user to use text and images, while others allow users to use images only. Examples of sites utilizing both text and images are Facebook, Twitter, and WhatsApp. In case you're a fan of images, you can use such sites like Instagram, Flickr, and Pinterest. This article aims at exploring the importance of this medium and how you can apply it to grow your profile and your audience as well.

Instagram is a social networking site that utilizes images only. The site allows users to upload pictures and videos which they can edit using available features. There are different reasons why you should use Instagram. These include:

- **Access to many users**- Globally, Instagram has more than 800 million users. This is a significant number, and as a business-minded person, you need to sign up on this platform so that you access some targeted audience.

- **Simplification of networking**- The site has features that make it easier for you to network with different people in accordance to their locale, hashtags, and interests. Using this site, you can develop an audience both in the local and international arena.

- **Reach**-Instagram has the capability of enabling you to reach a vast and active audience than Facebook and Twitter. This means that building your personal or business brand through Instagram is a critical step toward business success or expansion. Furthermore, Instagram allows you to engage with the audience by letting them comment about your products or creating new hashtags.

- **Simple to apply**-with Instagram, you can be able to communicate easily with people from all parts of the world by sharing photos and videos from wherever you'll be.

- **Pictures are a powerful means of communication**-many people like pictures. Therefore, because Instagram is picture-based, it's a great way of forming and engaging a targeted audience. A photo will communicate a lot within a short period than text.

- **Connections**-Instagram offers you an opportunity to connect with a vast number of people that have the same interest as yours. Research has shown that many people are actively engaged in this platform most of the time, in comparison with other platforms such as Facebook and Twitter. Therefore, using this medium, you're likely to socially connect with many people at both the local and global arena.

- **Business feel**-Many top and small brands are likely to be found on Instagram than other platforms, including Facebook and WhatsApp.

- **Visual appeal**-Pictures speak a lot within a short time. Many people prefer stories told through photos than those offered in text form. This is because photos are simple to read than going through a text.

- **Suitable for all businesses**-this platform suits all types of businesses, whether small or big. In this connection, you have the chance to promote yourself through this medium.

How to Grow Your Profile On Instagram

One significant advantage of Instagram is that it offers you an opportunity to expand your business through a targeted audience. The target audience is one that is interested in whatever services or products that you offer. In case you want to grow your profile through Instagram, there are different tactics that you can apply. These include:

- **Profile**-on your Instagram account, you need to have an exceptional bio and that of your business captured. Ensure that your business' log is outstanding and will be able to attract a vast audience. To ensure that your profile photo is exceptional, ensure that you apply shades that capture your business mood, tone, and atmosphere.

- **Why you're here**-It's essential to inform your audience why you're using this platform. In this regard, you intend to make the audience connect with your brand.

- **Importance of a strategy**-the aim of using any social media platform is to grow your business. Before you start posting images on this site, it's essential to have a business plan. This plan should indicate the stage at which your business will begin posting photos on this site and what intention or objective you would like to achieve.

- **Application of hashtags**-when using hashtags, it's essential to let your business voice come out instead of allowing them to be your voice. Through hashtags, your brand voice must be heard. When you want to be successful in using hashtags, it's essential to make sure that they're relevant and should be applied sparingly. Conducting some background research is vital. Such kind of study will enable you to generate the best hashtags and those that many of your followers will give likes. Two key tools will assist you in selecting the relevant hashtags. These include Websta and Instagram bots. The bottom line is to make sure that your audience likes the hashtags that you use.

- **Images**-what will enable you to succeed in promoting your profile through Instagram is the kind of photos that you use. In this regard, it's advisable to apply the relevant features of Instagram to beautify your images.

- **Be different**-To be successful in this platform; you must always strive to be distinguishable. You need to ensure that you use specific styles that help to identify your brand from others. In this regard, it's advisable to use the same frame, filters, and other related techniques.

- **Sharing the content of your followers**-when you share content generated by your audience, they feel great. You can request your followers for these pictures for regramming. It's essential to give the audience content credit before sharing so that it does not look like your own generated content. When followers see their pictures shared in your Instagram account, they're likely to tag their friends, and through this approach, you increase your followers.

- **Knowledge about your audience**-to be successful in generating the best content; it's essential to understand your audience. Many users found on Instagram are the youth who like trendy and appealing content. It's crucial to carry out some background research about them to enable you to generate content which they'll identify with. For instance, in case you sell maternity clothes, your target audience is expectant mothers. Use the right terms to refer them so that they can connect with you at the emotional level. For example, you can address them as tomorrow's moms.

- **Telling moving stories**-Many people like stories. Through the caption space given, you can tell a story about your image. Let your audience know how you started your business and the challenges that you have faced on the way. These stories make the audience to identify with your brand. For example, you can post an image that captures a stage in your business when you found that moving forward was almost impossible because you never had funds. But because you had ideas, you want sponsorship that enabled you to overcome the challenge. This image will tell people that in spite of the difficulties and challenges, you can still overcome them and be successful in business.

- **Timing**-the time when you post your image is essential as it determines the number of people who will see it. For instance, consider uploading your pictures early in the morning on weekdays and throughout the day on weekends. In case you want to find out about the best time to post your content, it's essential to use Google Analytic tools.

- **Emotional connections**- people like content that they can easily connect with at the emotional level. In this regard, you should learn to personalize your content. You need to post material which features human beings to enable the audience to connect with you at the emotional level. Having an audience connecting with you at an emotional level will also have the same audience similarly connect with your business.

- **Reply to feedback**-It's essential to have your followers engaged by ensuring that you reply to their comments. Many people love it when you respond to their comments. It shows that you appreciate time by sparing some time to reply to what they're saying.

- **Be steadfast**-human beings do not like vacuums. In this regard, it's vital to ensure that you're consistent with your postings on Instagram. You need to avoid taking too long before you share content. You are expected to do it daily.

- **Be funny**-it's essential to avoid posting boring content. You need to be humorous and make the audience laugh through what you post. Avoid posting scholarly content on Instagram, as many people may not like it. You become more engaging when you post funny material, and many will share it. Just imagine how your day will be by coming across a funny story in the morning. You'll probably smile throughout the day. In case you want your brand to be memorable, always share fun content with your audience.

- **Using other platforms**-You can have more Instagram followers when you promote your Instagram content on other social media sites like Facebook and Twitter. The people who come across this content will go to your Instagram page, where they will find more content.

- **Strategic partnerships**-you can get more followers on Instagram by collaborating with brands that you have a lot in common. These brands will help you find more active audiences, which will enable you to take you're a business to another level. For instance, a telecom brand can team up with a bank to get more followers on Instagram.

- **Influencer partnerships**-Influencers in your industry can act as brand ambassadors who will spread the word about your business and enable you to have more followers on your Instagram. It's important to develop partnerships with them.

- **Photo competition**-you can have photo contests where you ask participants to capture their best images and post them on your Instagram page. Through these contests, you need to ask the participants to tag their friends. If you inform the participants that the best image will receive an award, they're likely to tell more people to start following you. In this regard, you increase your audience.

- **Optimization of your profile**- to make sure that your profile is highly optimized, ensure that you use a precise lower case Instagram handle. Additionally, apply a relevant image, use the right keywords, and put down the best bio.

- **Tagging people**-One way of growing your followers through Instagram is through tag people. Those tagged will be excited and will start following you.

- **Knowledge about your competitors**- It's essential to understand your competitors so that you can attract the audience from them. You need to conduct some background research about your rivals to understand them.

- **Encourage followers to act**-You can post an exciting photo and ask followers to like it and tag a friend. By encouraging your followers to act, you're likely to increase your audience.

- **Creation of a theme for your content**- It's essential to have an idea for your images. For example, if you're a wedding photographer, you can use such themes as lovely, gorgeous, etc.

- **Like other people's content and follow them**-People are likely to reciprocate your gesture. When you like their content, give a helpful comment and start following them, they'll also start doing so on your side. You should not expect people to start following you if you don't support them.

- **Behind the scenes photos**-in those industries where people don't understand what takes place behind the scenes, you can occasionally share photos on how you operate behind the scenes. These kinds of content will attract many followers.

Chapter 6: Tips to Get the Most Out of Any Instagram Profile

Innovations of new applications are nowadays happening daily. Social media apps are the most sought after all over the world. Instagram is one of the most downloaded apps, as it's free and allows its users to share videos and photos captured. Facebook acquired it, another popular social media app barely two years after its creation. Corporate entities and small, medium-sized enterprises have taken into Instagram to grow their market bases.

The social apps need to upgrade often to stay on top of the game, and that's why Instagram presents new features regularly. Popularity is a factor to be considered to remain relevant. The numerous features introduced into the app might create some difficulty for some who want to use it. Below are some of the tips generated to help people get the most out of Instagram profiles and boost a brand.

1. **Consistency in uploading Stories and Posts**

The Instagram story feature can enable app users to assemble stories in their profile by sharing pictures or videos taken. The story is made more attractive by adding effects, tunes, and even texts to it. The uniqueness of the Instagram story is the visibility duration. The story uploaded automatically disappear after 24 hours of its upload time. The regular Instagram post will, however, remain visible, and so when creating a brand, one needs to continuously upload on Instagram stories at best once in a day. This practice will enable one to maintain his/her relevance.

For the regular Instagram post, one needs to be uploading daily. Missing to post for days doesn't do justice to the brand you trying to create. 'Out of sight, out of mind' ideology applies in this scenario. It's a matter of creating a routine and sticking to it.

The Instagram Stories feature has numerous advantages for influencers and organizations exploiting it. The following are some of the positivity of the feature;

It can be utilized in capturing behind-the-scenes of projects carried out by brands or influencers as it does not require the attentiveness to details, worthiness as the regular Instagram uploads.

It has various features that make it more fun to use, such as sounds and filter effects.

The Instagram stories exhibited on top of followers' timeline, and hence it's the first thing one sees when it opens the app.

Stories prominently displayed at the top of follower timelines just under the Instagram logo.

The feature as its limits and one being, its availability is limited to mobile apps. The Instagram story element can be sent to a follower as a message directly to his/her app inbox.

2. Create a brand that is associated with positivity

The only people around Instagram that have a readymade fan base are celebrities, while others start from the bottom. Individuals and enterprises need to follow hashtags that bring out their visions and goals they would want their brand associated with by potential clients. For instance, a football fan can follow, like, and comment on photos or hashtags that are relevant to the sport. Creating a sneakers shop? Follow and discuss users' sneaker collection and advice of the fashion. Through this engagement, a user can turn from being a follower to a client. Don't let out people to view you as desperate for attention, which will only push them away.

3. Getting to use swipe up feature in the app

This is one of the welcomed features of using Instagram as a marketing tool. It allows followers to 'swipe up.' Organizations brands and social media influencers who have thousands of followers can use the feature to their advantage. It involves adding a link to a website. The direct link created will automatically become visible to any person who swipes up. Through this, visitors are directed to brand webpages generating traffic. Brands and influencers can market their products and content.

4.   Promoting creativity while marketing contents and work done

Brands need to emphasize the results of their ability to offer and not the product it is making. It's vital to add value to followers and potential clients while maintaining a perfect image. Creating a brand that is associated with good things of high quality adds value to the organization. A positive perspective is also vital and visual content.

If the business operations are in the hospitality sector, emphasis needs to put on practices carried out behind the scenes of hospitality. The organization's goals, mission, and visions can be brought out to the world by creating videos of employees demonstrating the organization's culture.

5.   Going with followers behind-the-scenes

Studies have shown clients and followers have a high level of interest associated with knowing how the items they use created and the process involved. With the Instagram app, the company's clients and followers can be shown what is required. The followers will feel appreciated and part of the enterprise when such tactics are employed. Photos of meetings and how employees are brainstorming can be uploaded and engaging the followers in the comment section. When different images are uploaded with different captions, one is likely to catch the eye of followers hence generate traffic. There is no need for deleting photos or videos that didn't get attention as they can be archived instead.

6.   Using hashtags to grow on followers and market base

Hashtags can be used in developing the brand and being able to reach many people. Motivations for such hashtags can be different such as advertising a launched product, campaigns for existing items, and also campaigns for a course. The hashtags need to realistic and bring out day to day activities of an ordinary individual. The course name can be used as a hashtag or the company's name.

It enables individuals to get your platform quickly when trying to find products associated with the brand and the account.

It's generally recommended that one uses between four to six hashtags in the caption sector even though the limit is 30 under an upload. The trending hashtags can also be used to reach a wider audience such as the #mcm, #tbt, and #wcw are some of the most popular hashtags visited.

7. **Coming together in the form of collaborations and tagging others**

The platform created by the Instagram app is so massive it's used in showcasing different partnerships done by brands and influencers. Success, contributions, and philanthropic stories can be shared across the world. When companies partner in giving back to society, it can be highlighted. Tagging accounts that are associated with such acts is also a plus as through that, you also tap into its broad audience, making you noticed.

Brands and influencers also use another means to help grow their audience by employing 'shout outs.' The practice enables both accounts to tap to each other's audience hence impacted positively. There are two types of a shout out, namely paid and unpaid. Unpaid shout out involves different accounts with the generally same number of followers, and so the act is benefiting both of them. Paid shout out includes an account with a much bigger audience than the other. The more significant account is funded by the brand to promote its products or services offered and even gain followers in the event.

8. **Create a sense of suspense and uniqueness**

The art of making your followers and clients wanting more from your brand is a positive tool. Create an environment that the followers are always and eager waiting for uploads. When the company is rolling out new products or services, it makes the customers the first to know via social media. Creating short Instagram stories that make them want more information about the story. Rewarding followers' once in a while through campaigns is the best way to make people following you have an impression of superiority.

9. **Making use of the various video formats available in Instagram**

As the saying goes, a picture is worth a thousand words; some belief in modern society videos are worth even more. The social media app has different video formats that can be utilized by Instagram users for advertising. For instance, the Instagram stories can be used to stream live events and meetings and also recorded versions. It also has the option of mashing up videos form a one-minute time format in single videos. The Instagram stories support the vertical full-screen video format. Photos and videos can be merged into one to produce a very captivating ad.

10. **Using film subtitles and closed captions**

The majority of people prefer video to audio, and that's why Instagram users typically mute sound while viewing the video. For these particular reasons, brands can employ the use of subtitles to pass the intended message. Studies carried out as shown that a video that has a caption has a 13% increase viewership than a non-captioned video. Videos that have subtitles also have a higher possibility of being viewed compared to one that has only audio.

11. **Use GIFs feature**

It has been observed that people tend to watch up to the end of shorter videos, 20 seconds, and below. This is where brands can utilize the GIFs feature to their advantage. Most people find GIFs more attractive than images. There are two formats of GIFs, namely PNG and JPEG. This feature is more attractive because it's less expensive and also doesn't consume too much time compared to videos.

With this idea in mind, Instagram developers introduced the Boomerang. The Boomerang entails recording a bit continuous sequence, bringing it together then lopping it repeatedly.

12. **Profile Bio Creativity**

The Instagram bio is whereby individuals can sell themselves or brand to the public by showing what your work is and details about you. One can also take the opportunity to add more details to it by starting the hobbies and entertaining part of their lives. It's all for fun and entertainment, and lots of seriousness doesn't cut it out for followers.

Some of the best ways to bring out the creativity in the Instagram bio of individuals is through;

· Employing the use of Emoji in text spacing

This is the most used technique of spacing texts in a bio. By integrating the use of Emoji, it's able to bring out colorfulness in rather a dull bio and also the fun bit. Emoji creating have made the social apps be more attractiveness to also messaging impact can easily portray. Emojis can show one's personality, fun factor, country, and state of mind.

· Using different fonts in the bio

The popularity of this technique has dwindled in time. Though it used to be the best way of being unique from other people's bios. There are third-party apps that can be used to help generate a spectacular font for Instagram bios.

· Line breaks

By coming up with line breaks in a bio can be useful by bringing in a bit of formality. It creates a sense of authenticity in a bio enabling you to stand out in the profile. The line break feature is only visible in mobile apps.

· Having a Call-to-Action in a brands Instagram Bio

Having a call-to-action is vital to the brand one wants to create. Your followers can distinguish your brand from others by knowing your call-to-action, especially in a scenario, it is appealing. Catchy phrases can significantly improve followers' engagement with the brand.

· Indicating location and working hours

When the location of the company is known, it can help potential clients to reach it quickly. The working hours also give people more information about the organization. The information displayed in the bio can be used by customers and also reach a wider audience.

·   Create a link in your Instagram bio to your website

When the traffic in your Instagram account is high, one can use this to his/her advantage. A website link can be placed in the bio. The link can be made more attractive by offering rewards and promotions to the followers who decide to visit the site. The Instagram traffic also generates websites traffic make it more beneficial to influencers and brands.

Chapter 7: Using Paid Advertising on Instagram to Grow Your Reach

In this chapter, you will learn about paid advertising on Instagram, its cost as well as the various ways it can be done. You will also learn about advertising via Instagram stories and why it is useful. Read on to find out!

How Much Do Instagram Ads Cost?

The average cost per click for Instagram ads is around $0.70 to $0.80. However, the cost of your specific ad will depend on your budget because not all ads are the same. The estimated cost comes from an analysis done on over $300 Million spent on ads in a certain period.

You should note that the estimated figure is just the average cost-per-click, your ads might cost less more than that or more depending on various factors. Several Instagram advertisers find the ads to have very high engagement, but it comes at a cost. Keith Baumwald, the founder of Leverage Consulting, says that Instagram ads are slightly more expensive compared to Facebook ads, but worth it given the fact, their conversation rate is very high. Instagram ads provide advertisers with the opportunity to control how the budgets are allocated. For example, you can choose how much you can spend in a single day by setting daily limits. You can also set the total amount to be paid over a certain period until the budget is depleted.

Some of the other ways you can control the budget include setting up an ad schedule that can specify certain hours of the day you prefer your ads to run. You can also set your ad delivery method as well as setting the bid amount.

Why Instagram Advertising Is Good for Your Business

So many people are using Instagram. A recent survey showed that there over 1 Billion Instagram users. With such a high number of users, there are no limits to what your business can archive through ads.

Any business can thrive on Instagram irrespective of the size. Right advert strategies will always deliver on your business needs. Instagram advertising can also enable you to earn money directly. Instagram has a greater emphasis on generating high revenue through product placement. They recently rolled out a platform called Shoppable Posts that allows businesses to add links to their post ads that include the price, shop now button, and the product description often influences users to buy the product.

How to Advertise On Instagram

For beginners, advertising on Instagram might seem very complicated, but if you've advertised on Facebook before, there isn't much to learn. Instagram ads can be configured through the Facebook Ad Manager. If you've never advertised on Facebook previously, don't fret, I will take you through the process below.

In this article, I'll focus on creating ads through the Facebook Ad Manager, which is the most popular method thanks to its ease-of-use and the ability to customize your ads. Follow the steps below to create your Instagram ad!

1. Go to Facebook's Ad Manager

The first step is going to the Ad Manager on Facebook. You can do so by simply following a link assuming you've logged in to the appropriate Facebook account.

You might be asking yourself, why use Facebook's Ad Manager, yet you want your ad on Instagram? The reason is that there is no specific Ad manager for Instagram; all Instagram ads are managed through the Facebook Ads UI.

2.Set Your Marketing Objective.

This is one of the most important steps when doing an Instagram ad. It is the main reason you decide to sponsor your ad; do you need more website traffic? Are you looking to increase product awareness? You have the liberty to set the objective of your ad. Let's have a look at each of the possible purpose and what it means.

-**Brand Awareness:** This is the most standard objective that will show your ads to potential customers likely to be interested in your product or service. This objective is undoubtedly going to expose your brand to relevant folks.

-**Reach:** This is the number of people your post reaches; it's more of the number of people that see your ads in their feed. The best thing about this objective is that it takes advantage of Facebook's split testing feature, which allows you to split your ad test into two and find out which one yields more conversation.

-**Traffic:** If you are looking to lead more readers to your website or more people to the app store so as they can download your app, this is the objective you should opt for. You can, therefore, choose one between the two and let the traffic jam in.

-**Engagement:** if you want more likes, comments shares, and overall engagement, you should go for the engagement objective. You should, however, note that you can only pay for "post engagement " on Instagram. Facebook will allow both "page engagement" and "event responses," an option currently unavailable to Instagram

-**App Installs:** This is the objective you should opt for if your goal is to increase your app downloads from the app store. You'll, however, have to choose your app from the app store during the setup.

-**Video Views;** This objective is very straightforward and doesn't need additional set up.

-**Lead Generation**: If you need more leads, this is the objective you should go for. Note that lead generation ads don't provide the same pre-filled fields as those on Facebook. Instagram supports phone numbers, email, full name, and gender.

-**Conversions:** This objective allows you to drive your potential customers to take action and convert on your website or your app. You must configure either an app or a Facebook pixel based on the site you're looking to promote. This allows you to track your conversions.

3. Configure Your Target Audience.

After selecting your objective, you need to come up with an appropriate target audience for your ad. This is easy to do because you'll use Facebook's demographic depth to reach the right people. Below are some of the aspects you should consider when configuring your audience.

Location: Allows you to target a country, state, region, city, zip code, exclude or include specific places, among other considerations.

Age: It allows you to target the specific ages of people from 13 to 65+

Gender: Some products and services are only meant for a single-gender; this will allow you to specify that.

Language: This is useful when you want to focus only on people that speak a specific language. Facebook, however, recommends leaving this option out.

Interests: This is usually under detailed targeting. It is meant to reach out to people interested in certain products and activities. For instance, if your ad talks about beverages, your target should be people interested in drinks and refreshments!

4. Choose Your Placements

After targeting your audience, it's time you learned about choosing your placements. This is the step where you'll decide where you want your ads to appear, on Facebook or Instagram. If you ignore this step, your adds will appear on both platforms. This isn't necessarily a bad thing, but if your ad was specifically meant for Instagram, you should select the "Edit Placements" option.

5.Set Your Budget and Ad Schedule.

This is the step where your financial power comes into play. How much do you want to spend on the ads? For how do you want the ads to run? You can control your expenses by pausing or stopping the campaign anytime you feel like your budget isn't being correctly allocated.

You can run the ad schedule to target specific times and days of the week, especially those times when you feel most users are active on the platform.

6. Creating Your Instagram ad.

After learning all the necessary steps, it's now time you create your Instagram ad! At this time, you already have an idea in mind for the ad you're looking to promote. To clarify some of the things you might find confusing, let's discuss the various types of ads!

Types of Instagram Ads

Instagram offers various formats of ads, from stories ads to Carousel. Each of these ad formats is placed in the user's feed and stories in a captivating way. Let's look at each of these ad formats and see how they work.

1. Instagram Stories Ads.

These are 25-hour self-destructing photo and video streams almost similar to Snapchat stories. Instagram Stories Ads allows you to insert an ad in between the user's stories. It fits the format of an Instagram story keeping the user experience flow uninterrupted and consistent.

This kind of ads can be composed of a single photo or video of up to 15 seconds. For maximum conversion, use high-quality media, whether you opt for a video or picture. Photo ads last only for 5 seconds, while video ads last for up to 15 seconds. Once viewed, users aren't able to return to it like a regular story meaning it can only be viewed once.

2. Photo Ads

 Photo ads allow you to showcase products and services through attractive images. You should use images that sell your product or service without accompanying it with words. It is advisable to use colored images as plain ones won't lead to reasonable conversion rates.

3. Video Ads

Research shows that in 2018, Instagram users spent significantly more time watching videos compared to the previous year. Businesses can tap this market and package their ads in the form of videos. You should, however, be very specific with your target audience as some users won't bother watching your video, especially if they can't relate to your product or service.

4. Carousel Ads

This kind of ads lets Instagrammers swipe through a series of videos or images with a call button to connect directly with you. This type of advertisement is perfect for brands that want to show the versatility of their products.

5. Collection Ads

It was introduced in early 2018. These ads combine the power of videos, photos, and direct response marketing in one great ad.

Collection Ads have been used mostly in situations where both video and photos are needed. They are instrumental and been known to produce high conversations. The cost is based on the number of clicks on your post and the total amount of time your videos have been viewed.

Chapter 8: Incredible Ways to Make Money on Instagram

In this social media era, opportunities to create an extra stream of income are unlimited. We've got bloggers, influencers, and YouTubers who are already cashing in big on their social media exploits. Fortunately, social media is a playing ground without many restrictions. All you need to excel on social media is great content.

People prefer to be on different social media platforms. The choice depends on their taste and preferences. Instagram is one of the platforms that have a significant number of active users. If you have thought of making some money on social media, there are a lot of opportunities on Instagram.

In this piece, we are going to show you how you can monetize your Instagram account. At the end of it, you will have acquired enough knowledge to start earning revenue on Instagram.

How Many Followers Should You Have To Make Money On Instagram?

Some of the popular Instagrammers have thousands of followers. While it would be great to have such a following, it is not necessary to start making money. Therefore, you don't need to have a staggering following to monetize your Instagram account.

As you know, there are many fake followers on Instagram. What you need are engaged followers and a high degree of commitment. If you've already got that, all you need to think about is ways to make money on Instagram. Fortunately, you don't have to look further as you are already in the right place.

Quality content is a prerequisite to earning revenue on Instagram. With that being said, it is imperative that upload top-notch content on your Instagram page. Use clear videos and images. It helps if your content speaks the same language. As this will create a much-needed brand identity. You can't be the jack of all trades on

Instagram. For example, if you combine fashion, travel, and fitness content, you are likely to confuse your audience.

Ways To Make Money On Instagram

1. Affiliate Marketing

Affiliate marketing revolves around promoting products for a select brand on your account. And whenever your efforts lead to a sale, you get a certain percentage of the profits. This is a popular practice among bloggers. But it also works well on social media.

So, how can you start your affiliate marketing campaign on Instagram?

The first step is to find a brand that could use your services. This will depend on what your Instagram page is all about. For example, if your interest is fashion, then you can work with a fashion store that needs to promote various products.

What follows is taking quality photos of the products you want to promote. Upload the images on your Instagram, including the affiliate link provided by the brand. Irresistible images are instrumental in driving sales. You should never compromise on that. Get it right, and you'll get paid.

Remember, an affiliate link has to appear on every image of the products you intend to promote. The URL can either be included in your bio or in captions. Long affiliate links aren't the best. It is prudent to keep them as short as possible. Use Bit.ly to shorten your links and make them appealing.

How to choose the right affiliate marketing opportunities

As we pointed out earlier, numerous companies offer affiliate marketing opportunities. You have to choose the brand you want to work strategically. Look for a company that corresponds to your niche. You'll undoubtedly have a better chance of succeeding with such a brand. Moreover, you'll understand each other and easily grind out a way forward in your dealings.

For example, if your audience follows you because you give them fitness tips, work with companies that sell fitness products. The objective is to promote products that are relevant to the content that appeals to your audience on Instagram.

Additionally, there are affiliate marketplaces that can help you get started. These include ClickBank, MaxBounty, ShareAsale, and so on.

2. Create Sponsored Posts

You've probably heard of social media influencers. This is people who have built a massive following on social media by posting content that drives engagement. Their audience views these people as trends-setters or reputable experts on particular niches. They are an authority and whichever product they endorse; consumers are convinced that it is the best in the market.

Ever since the rise of influencers, brands have found partnering with them to be tremendously lucrative. This happens through sponsored posts that help promote their products.

You may think that such companies are only interested in the size of your audience. However, that's far from the truth. The level of engagement with your audience means a lot to them. A closely knitted audience that shows immense interest in your content is quite desirable. Besides that, such an audience is good for business. If you have 1000 followers who show immense interest in your page, there is a chance of monetizing your account.

How much should I get paid for the sponsored posts?

As you decide on how much you want to get paid per post, it is important to consider that you'll have to create the content. This could be videos, images, or text. The brand you are posting for may also be interested in using your content elsewhere, such on their website. You'll be offering a complete advertising package.

You can either charge per single post or for the whole campaign. Additionally, you can opt to be paid with a free product or a fee. It all depends on how you negotiate with your client. Sometimes you may charge a fee and also get yourself a free product. If at all you use their products, and it's quality satisfactory, then you shouldn't have a problem pushing it in the market place.

As much as this sounds simple, you'll undoubtedly be offering great value to your client. They'll have access to an audience that you've created through your efforts. You will also give up the rights to your account for a set period. You deserve to be well compensated for what you are bringing on board.

If you play your card rights, you can charge from $150 to $400 per post. If you've changed to a business account, this may help you to negotiate for a higher rate.

How to find brands to partner with?

For a reputable influencer, you probably don't have to do much to get clients. They will find you. However, you can't just rely on being found. You need to put yourself out there. Other ways to find brands to work with include listing yourself on influencers' marketplaces. Also, you can directly pitch some of the brands that interest you.

Some of the places to list your account as influencer include Grapevine and Fohr Card. It is imperative that you notify your audiences as far as sponsored posts are concerned. This helps to maintain the trust and integrity you have built over time.

3. Selling Pictures

Instagram is a great platform to showcase both digital images and photographs. It gets better than that if you have high-quality pictures, as you can sell them.

As you are aware, there are plenty of pictures being posted on Instagram daily. Anyone who has a Smartphone can take pictures of whatever they like and post. This means that if you are going to promote and sell pictures on Instagram, they've got to be special. Expect that the competition will be stiff. Whatever you put out there, make certain that it's the best.

It doesn't matter whether you are a professional photographer or not. The one thing you must do is offer exquisite and unique pictures. There are many ways to achieve this. For instance, if you love to travel to world-renown destinations, you can take distinctive pictures and showcase them on your Instagram page. This may include pictures of a wildlife species that are not found within your continent.

Pick a niche such as travel; take pictures that would interest your audience. Pictures are universal. This means you have a lot to work with across various industries.

How to reach customers

Instagram makes it easy to reach customers. You can create a portfolio of pictures on your page to showcase your photography prowess. Ensure that you upload high-quality images.

When you have built a great portfolio, you can message your potential customers directly. Moreover, you can direct any inquiries to your Instagram page. This could be traffic from your website or blog if you've got one.

To take it a notch higher, convert your Instagram account into a business account. This will allow you to add your contact details to your account. People don't have all the time to find what they want. Make it easy to be contacted.

If you decide to sell your images in the form of print on online stores, then Instagram can come in handy in terms of promoting your pictures.

To give your work more exposure, you can sign up with some of the most popular market places. These include Foap, Snapwire, and Twenty20. Proceed to promote your content from these market places on Instagram.

4. Promote your Services, Products or Business

Another effective way to make money on your Instagram account is to promote your products, services, or business.

If you own a business, then you have a clear idea of the kind of audience you'd like to sell to. The challenge lies in how to reach them. Your past sales can help you identify the customers you should target in your Instagram promotion efforts.

Your bio should be on point in terms of describing what your business is all about. Follow this up by numerous picturesque shots of your products.

One of the most powerful ways to market your products is by posting pictures of your customers with them. This should be done with their consent. Your prospects are likely to get a good feeling about your products when they see happy customers posing with them. For example, seeing a customer enjoy a piece of chicken on a KFC may appeal to your appetite. The next time you want to enjoy some chicken, you will undoubtedly have KFC on your mind.

The same case applies to your products. If you sell customized t-shirts, have a willing happy customer's share a photo wearing one of your pieces. This is the kind of advertising appeals to your potential customers as well as drive sales.

When it comes to services, infographics work wonders. Create clear, attractive infographics that promote your services. This is a great way to notify your audience of the best offers as well as discounts. Feature the infographics on Instagram, either in the form of stories of single posts.

The freedom of creativity that Instagram offers could be pivotal in boosting your sales. It allows you to represent your brand uniquely.

5. Sell Advertising Space on your Instagram Page

When you boast a significant following on Instagram, various brands will be interested in advertising on your page. Specializing in a particular niche makes you an authority in your chosen field.

For instance, if you are an authority in fitness with a considerable following, you can sell advertising space to companies that sell fitness products. Such products may include supplements, clothes, equipment, and so on.

Attracting clients that would be interested in advertising on your Instagram page is not easy. Your page has to be loaded with insightful and relevant content. Brands that want to work with you have to view your Instagram presence as valuable.

6. Become a Brand Ambassador

Becoming a brand ambassador is not the easiest way to make money on Instagram. But if you get it right, it could be a very lucrative venture. Before we delve more into it, let us learn more about brand ambassadors.

So, who is a brand ambassador?

A brand ambassador is someone who works as a brand representative in a select market place. The responsibility of a brand ambassador is to promote the business. A brand ambassador could be a customer who previously recommended a particular brand's products or services to others.

That is, however, not the only way to become a brand ambassador. If you command a massive following on Instagram, companies may appoint you to be their brand representative on Instagram. The company directs its brand ambassador on important aspects, such as how to interact with customers.

As a brand Instagram ambassador, you may be required to work with the company's marketing department. One of your responsibilities may be to endorse the company's product through your Instagram page. This can be done by posting pictures of the company's best-selling products.

How to become an Instagram brand ambassador

The first thing is to create a brand identity. You ought to have a personality on Instagram. Besides that, ensure that you have images with a cohesive flow. Your content should not be confusing. It should preach the same message. For this reason, the majority of your content must correspond with particular interests.

A wealth of content revolving around a specific interest gives you authority as a brand. It shows that your Instagram followers have chosen you because of your content. This is the kind of recognition you need to reach the heights of a brand ambassador.

Before you pitch a particular brand, ensure that your content is befitting to the company's core business. Also, let the brand know what makes you the best brand ambassador for their business. The activity on your account, as well as the size of your audience, should be convincing.

How to get clients

After satisfying the entire requirement that makes a brand ambassador, send a pitch to your potential clients. Get in touch with various brands across your niche. As soon one accepts to work with you, you'll be generating an income through your Instagram account.

7. Sell Your Instagram Account

Do you feel like your Instagram account has reached its peak? Maybe you have created a great audience in a particular niche and would like to pursue something else. You may have figured out that the experience you have acquired is enough to help you create a better Instagram presence.

If that's the case, then you need to move on from your current Instagram account. With all the work that you put behind building your account, your efforts should not go in vain. Perhaps you could sell it.

Go to Viral accounts or Fame swap. These are websites that help you sell social media accounts. If yours is worth the salt, you can cash it for a good price.

As you can see, you can turn your Instagram account into a cash cow. If you meet the criteria described in this chapter, you should already be generating revenue on Instagram. Remember that once you decide to make money on Instagram, the account should maintain a great level of professionalism without losing its golden touch. Be careful with what you post so that you can avoid putting your page in jeopardy. Good luck!

Chapter 9: How to convert your Instagram Followers into Buyers

Instagram, like any other social media platform, has been turned into a business growing mode. Most businesses people use it as a way of interacting or posting pictures, but it does more than that. As many followers you have, you can, as well as turn them into potential buyers of your products. You may need to create awareness of your product, brand, or your services, and convince your followers that they should buy what you are offering. Recently, Instagram has received a good rating for improving businesses and creating profit. However, it is not easy as ABC as it takes lots of work, skills, and tips on getting a potential buyer on your side.

Before getting the buyer to trust or listen to what you are talking about, you need to have a good business strategy. This will help them make up their mind on buying what you are selling or not. It takes a lot of effort, and you need to provide all the information about your product or services and give the buyer an insight into what they may be missing if they don't buy or how they will be impacted. Most companies and organizations have taken Instagram by storm, and they are using campaigns and innovative ways of getting a large following. A following without supporting your idea is worthless, but that may be the start you need. You can turn them into potential buyers by using creative marketing strategies that will arouse their curiosity in knowing what you are offering.

Instagram can be the best avenue for your growth, but getting your followers to like what you are selling and deciding on buying your products and services may be challenging. You may need to sacrifice more than posting your products and explaining to your followers about your brand. You can, however, seek the help of social media managers who can help you turn your followers' likes into a purchase or monetize your product on Instagram. However, this does not guarantee you instant results or positive feedback. You will have to invest more and think outside the box to maintain a healthy relationship with your followers to build trust for an easier approach.

To make your followers more attracted to buy your products, you can try these simple tips:

Be Unique

Every other company or business wants to turn its followers into buyers, and they will employ the same strategies in driving them to their side. As much as it may work, you need to be different. Your potential buyers need to feel the need to try your brand as it has something the other brands do not provide. They will be interested in buying your products to experience the difference.

Here, you need to use creative and innovative business ideas to attract the attention of your buyers. For example, using the same content for your brand or product may become boring as there would be nothing different about it. People tend to be moved by what they see. If they see one thing or idea from Monday to Monday, they will definitely lose interest in associating with it. That is the same thing with promoting your products. You may need to invest in different ideas to make it more attractive. People will get attracted to new things, and they will feel the need to wait and see what lies beneath the product and experience it.

You can invest in artists to create fresh content all the time for your brand unique and worthwhile. Presenting your product or service in a different way helps the follower feel you are serious about the product you are selling. You can decide on using videos, series, or stories updates describing what you are selling, and that will make your followers yearn for more updates daily, and that may turn their mind into buying them.

Rewards And Promotions

Who wouldn't love buying products at lower and affordable prices? This is an easy tip for turning your potential buyers into buyers. People will normally be attracted to rewards. They will feel motivated to get the value for their money from purchasing your products and services. They need to feel you care, and they can benefit from buying your product.

You can promote your products by giving a discount code for your followers to use within a specific time and sensitize it as an Instagram-only offer. This is very important as most of your followers will crowd on your page to make use of the offers by buying your products. You can consider using attractive offers such as 'buy one get one free,' 'buy all products for half its price' and so on. Within the given time frame, you will notice massive buying as people do not want to be left out. You can use this tip from time to time to make your followers visiting your page for more juicy deals and offers.

Improve Your Customer Service

Growth in business means there is a happy customer somewhere. You need to ensure your buyer is happy and satisfied with your services to make them come back. Good treatment will make your buyer feel that you care, and your products or brand is worth the value for their money. You can use a strategy to provide them with a warranty.

Your followers, come buyers will always get attracted to where the deal is good. They need to feel your products will meet their standards and that they are safe in case they meet technical or mechanical challenges on the way. Offering a longer warranty will guarantee your buyers protection, and that is what they need. They will develop trust, and that is a good thing for your business. They will compare the warranty of other companies and businesses and feel free to try yours.

There are cases you can promise your buyers a money-back guarantee in case the product does not reach their quality standards or is not what they wanted. Here, your potential buyer may experience your good customer service and go ahead to make the purchase without worrying about security as they are assured of the best products that will work, and if not they can return them or given another.

Stay Active On A Regular Basis

This is an important pick. Your followers need to feel your presence on your social media platforms to ascertain your seriousness. Being active will help you solve your followers' issues regarding your products or brand. They may have questions on promotions and discounts or how to get your products, where to get you, and more about how your products work.

In most cases, your Instagram followers may also be following you on other platforms. Responding to their comments in a more friendly and clear way may increase their chances of wanting to buy your brand. Having reliable customer care will improver your rating on social media as your potential buyers will be more drawn to transact with you.

Expand Your Territories In Marketing Channels

This tip will have a positive effect on your awareness. You will have more channels to sell your brand or product. You will be able to reach a large number of people and increase your following. The more the followers you have, the more your product becomes known.

Once you have established a massive following, you can now work on turning them to buyers by giving all the information that will benefit them once they consider buying your products. Ensure to post content that is of high quality to not only increase your following and likes but to attract your potential buyers to buy your brand. Posting mediocre content will always affect your brand, and that may lead to a decrease in followers or potential business growth. You should make sure not to ignore or rely on one platform. The more the platforms, the more the opportunity for your future endeavors.

Target Your Audience

As you try to make your following into buyers, ensure you know who your audiences are. You should establish a link between your followers and understand the impact your brand will have on them. You should make use of the right platform in addressing a different kind of people. On Instagram, you will mostly notice its users are young people.

In most cases, business people and companies make mistakes by concentrating on the products or selling their brands without giving their audience part of the content. They use the platform to describe the positive side of their goods and services without describing the effects it would have on the user. You should ensure you convince your audience that what you are selling is what they need and are looking for. Giving a clear picture of what it would add to the customers' lives or save the situation may be of greater advantage.

Be different and target your followers' needs and the kind of people you need the information to reach. For instance, if its young people you need, you can post it on Facebook and Instagram, and older people are easily found on twitter. Using your platform properly may increase your followers and more interest from your potential buyers accessing the products that meet their needs.

Continue Marketing Your Brand

It's quite unfortunate, we tend to think once your followers turn into buyers and your products are bought, it is the end of the game. That is not the case. As you will be presenting them with new products, you need to give them information and content that would captivate them into buying from you again.

You have to continue engaging and interacting with your customers offering them rewards and promotions once in a while to create a strong relationship. Doing it once and ignoring the news having reached your followers, you will be surprised not to have a single buyer. It should be a consistent stand. This will grow your followers' rate of visiting your page anytime you post about your products or brand.

Provide Information Clear And On Point

Always ensure you create enough awareness about your brand or product while going straight to the point. You do not have to exaggerate its features of advantages. Maintain a better relationship with your followers and give them content that is of high quality.

Information that will help them make a decision on choosing to buy from you. It should not be long posts but short and clear with a lot of weight.

You can give your contact information, where they can connect beyond Instagram, lead them to the right landing page for easy navigation. Whether they are online or not, they are able to buy your brand.

Be Original

Most people tend to trust more when they have an idea of who you are. You can give them a little background information on you, your family, and who you are in a real person. Copying other people can make some followers unfollow as they may be looking for something different from others. Being you may help drive in potential buyers as you will be more attracting. People mostly feel safe doing business or investing in people who they can trust, like, and know. It's always evident that people find it easy to associate with real people who are different and not normal or the same. Aim to being unique in how you market your brand as buyers will come to you.

Talk To Them

You can have a large number of followers, but you can easily communicate with them by commenting on their posts or sharing links regarding your brand and product. You can talk to them on a personal level by interacting with them. You can ask them to share your links or your story to their friends. That will help you get more followers and turn them into buyers. You can create videos of your brand and post it on your page. That can easily improve awareness and increase the number of visits to your page. You can post pictures of your brand on your social platforms and interact with them in the comments and answering their questions. You can also communicate one on one in case you have given out your contacts. You will turn your followers on your buyer side by simple communication.

It is important to focus and concentrate on growing your business or brand through Social media platforms. You can use tips such as talking to your followers and knowing your audience is a key feature. You can still maintain your buyers by being original and unique, as it will draw them to you. Once you have a potential buyer, continue marketing your brand and give precise information.

Chapter 10: Tips to Setting Up Your Instagram Account

In this chapter, you will learn about how you can set up your Instagram account, picking a name for your business profile, how to gain followers on Instagram as well as the kind of content you should publish. Read on to find out!

How to Set Up Your Instagram Account

Since its inception in 2010, Instagram has risen to become an integral medium for marketing. A recent study shows that there are over 1 billion Instagram users in the world today, making it the ideal platform for any business looking to grow and convert leads.

Instagram is used on phones, although you can also access the web version. So to use Instagram, you'll need an Android phone or iOS or Smart Tablet.

How can you sign up for Instagram? Upon installing the app, you will be prompted to either sign up for a new account or register with your Facebook account. When signing up for a business account, it is recommended you choose a relevant business email that matches all your social media accounts. This will ensure consistency and makes it easier for people to find your profile. An email gives a chance to customers who would like to get in touch to drop a mail that you can respond to swiftly.

Choosing A Username

When deciding on the username for the Instagram account, it is essential to keep it uniform across all the social media platforms. This creates consistency across all your platforms allowing users to recognize your brand with ease.

What about choosing a profile picture? This is the first thing a visitor to your profile will. The profile picture carries a lot of significance. It should be clear, crisp, and free from any clutter. If your business or organization has a logo, mascot, or acronym, you can use them as the profile picture in a clean background. Avoid using images that aren't associated with your business as profile pictures. It will be so awkward for your business that deals with automobiles to have a picture of Leo Messi or Cristiano Ronaldo as the profile picture.

How Do You Write an Excellent Instagram Biography?

When drafting your Instagram biography, it is essential to view it as a form of marketing and branding. This is one of the first things Instagrammers will see before scrolling down to your posts. It, therefore, should be captivating and add to your brand narrative, telling your visitors a little more about what you do, who you are, of what importance you can be to them as well as your contacts.

Instagram also lets you link one URL on your business profile. As a business, you should choose a link whose landing page is somewhere crucial concerning your sales strategies.

Connecting Instagram to Your Other Social Media Accounts

After setting up your Instagram account, you can now link it to your other social media accounts. The most popular social media platforms you can connect your Instagram account to are Facebook, Twitter, and LinkedIn. Linking these accounts will make it easy to share images and ensure uniformity.

Having set up all the basics about your Instagram account, it time you learned how you could drive traffic from your news feed through to your website.

How to Gain More Followers On Instagram

Your Instagram account can be very useless; it has no followers. Followers are people that can see your posts directly on in their feeds. It is therefore vital you gain followers before you go any further. For beginners, it can be very challenging to gain new followers. However, that shouldn't worry you because I will explain some of the methods you can increase your Instagram following. Read on to find out.

1. Use Hashtags

Hashtags are a popular feature on Instagram. You can even follow the hashtag that interests you the most. They are an easy avenue for your content to get noticed by other Instagram users you don't necessarily follow. For example, if you are an artist, adding hashtags on the type of musical instruments used in your image expands your pool of influence for other users who are interested in the same and don't follow you.

Hashtags can be broken down into three categories: let 's look at each one of them.

Brand and campaign hashtags

These hashtags can be used to promote brands and other campaigns. Brand hashtags can be a company name or a famous tagline. It is should always be relevant to your post because it can lose meaning and be rendered useless. Influential brands have used their famous slogans to help grow brand awareness and in the process, allow Instagrammers to adopt the tagline in their photos and videos.

Campaign hashtags, on the other hand, are almost similar to brand hashtags, but they more related to a particular topic that brand. When a football player has been racially abused, for example, a campaign hashtag like #SayNoToRacism can be used.

Trending Hashtags

These can be an excellent tool for marketing your business. They can only be relevant for a few hours, days, or weeks, but the traffic and followers you could get from it can stick around for a very long time. Examples of trending hashtag can be #Throwback, #MotivationMonday, among others. For them to be relevant, however, they should fit your niche. If your niche is about tiles and decor, you can use a hashtag like #InteriorDesign.

Content hashtags

These are tags that give more information about the content you are sharing. They can generate more conversion by leading people that don't follow you to your posts.

So exactly how can you gain followers using hashtags? This is how, first, you can start by following users you have common interests in; they more likely to follow you back.

You can also capitalize on the trending hashtags. These tags, in most occasions, have a high number of users seeing them, post your photo using the hashtag, and you are more likely going to gain yourself, new followers.

2. Connect it to other Social Media accounts

Connecting your Instagram account to other platforms like Facebook can help you increase your followers since 24% of your friends on Facebook are also Instagram users. It will help your friends discover you as an Instagram user and follow you immediately. As we discussed earlier, this is something you should do when setting up your profile. If any of your Facebook friends join Instagram, you will be alerted, and you will be able to follow them as well.

3. Join Instagram Engagement Groups

This technique is ideal for beginners. Newbies on Instagram have seen their followers increase tremendously by joining engagement groups. While it can be seductive to join large Instagram engagement groups, the fact is you'll gain a more targeted list of followers by sticking to what you do. There are various engagement groups from fashion, travel, beauty, and sports. From these groups, you can gain followers and likes from users who have similar interests. If they follow you, you should return the favor by following them back. This strategy can earn you up to 2000 followers within a short period. As much as it won't help you make immediate sales, it enables you to gain credibility, so your business account doesn't show you have very few followers. It is more of a short-term strategy for your first few days or weeks on Instagram.

4. Repost another user's content.

This will help you gain more followers in such a way that your profile will see by many more people. The trick here is that you should only repost engaging posts that are relatable to your niche. How do you know what to repost? Use hashtags. Browse the list of hashtags and find top-performing posts that haven't been posted by your competitor. Pick the one you feel can have high engagement and repost it.

5. Get Promoted on Buzzfeed

To gain more followers on Instagram, you will have to find a way to take advantage of a massive audience; no one can embed Instagram posts into their content as Buzzfeed does. If Buzzfeed isn't right for your niche, you can use other tools like HARO, where you can get connection requests from users interested in the same niche as yours.

6. Ask Your customers to share their photos

If you're still new on Instagram, gaining new followers can be more comfortable with customers' posts in your feed. This will help increase your social proof. Reach out to your customers and offer gifts for taking quality pictures with your product. The many customer pictures on your profile, the more interested people will be in your product. They will naturally start tagging your account in posts once they purchase them. If you like, comment and repost it, and follow them, they are more likely going to follow you back.

7. Follow People or Like their Photos

This is one of the most basic to gain followers. It's a way of getting people's attention by doing them service: like their photos or following them. According to a study, for every 100 pictures you like, it generates 25 likes on your photographs and gains you six new followers. There is no harm in following random Instagram users and banking on them to follow you back. Following other people stimulates curiosity them leading them to your profile. If your profile impresses them, there are high chances they will follow you back. Don't worry about having too many "following" before you get a significant number of followers first. You can always sort them out by using apps like intstafollow to find out who unfollowed you.

8. Have a Consistent Style

People don't follow you basing on the content you have already posted but because of what you are likely to post next. Let's say your account posts female shoes every day without fail; users will note you are more likely going to post again because your previous record shows consistency. So, they will follow you with the expectation that you'll share the same content.

Having a consistent theme isn't just about branding but about creating expectations for your account. If you can deliver with that consistency, you'll gain more followers on Instagram at a faster rate.

9. Work with Influencers

This is another way you can increase your Instagram followers. Get an influencer to give your profile a shout out or do an account take over. Influencers have a loyal following, asking them to follow your account is more likely going to yield fruits. They also have a high number of followers. You should, however, be careful to avoid influencers who can send fake traffic, this is because when your account gets a sudden rush of fake followers, it risks getting banned.

If you're seeking a more effective tactic, you can ask the influencer to take over your account.

10. Keep an eye out for what works.

When you come across a viral post, find out what it was about. You'll notice a pattern in the post. For example, if the tag is full of shoes and clothing with bright colors and sharp contrasts, try to have your version of such posts and see what happens. You should note that in this case, Instagrammers love photos that are beautiful and attractive. Random low-quality pictures of your dog, food, or drinks are not going to stand out. Try to be extremely selective when choosing which photo you want to upload.

11. Use Popular Filters

This shouldn't be your primary strategy, but you should give it a try. Popular filters can easily be identified by other users that like them and could trigger them to follow you. It is more of connecting with someone you have similar interests.

Chapter 11: Case Studies of Success on Instagram

There are several brands, businesses, and people who have used Instagram to grow and reach their potentials. It is not just a story; Instagram has propelled brands to reach more clients globally. Also, it has built businesses from scratches and even developed people's personal goals. That is, this thing is real, and it does work. However, some may become doubtful and say that they have tried, but it never worked. Maybe there are few things you missed, or you became impatient as getting the interest of others takes time. Check out these brands, businesses, and people who significantly succeeded when using Instagram.

Nike

The majority of all sports lovers around the world have come across the brand Nike more than once across different Media. One of them is Instagram, as with no doubt, millions of people have learned about their products. The brand has more than 90 million followers and directly among the top 20 most follower brands on Instagram. If Nike would have chosen to market through Television and radio advertisements, the chances are that only clients within the United States would learn about their product. This is because the company is an American footwear manufacturing company headquartered in Beaverton, Oregon, United States.

The massive online community, especially on Instagram, has enabled the company to handle an average of about 1,000,000 customer feedbacks each year. Nike uses a personalized approach to engage with the audience more so in the development of its consistency on social media. Every year, Nike experiences an increase of its online community, with each day having an average of between twenty and sixty following them on Instagram. The company has opted to assign a team that handles social media customers. Therefore, Nike is one of the brands on Instagram, which gained its successful from its social media presence.

Vans

Vans is another brand based in Costa Mesa, California, United States, with an Instagram follower of more than 17 million. When you visit all their social media pages, Vans primarily focuses on promoting its products with Instagram is not an exception. The brand is known for making classic checked slip-on with both standalone and action photo products. The news feeds have been viewed, commented, and liked by a vast Instagram community who are also their potential clients. That is, Van uses Instagram and other social media platforms to showcase and market their products.

In some cases, Van uses the most engaging Instagram feeds, with some being weirder and funny, but with a primary goal of promoting their products. More so, the company is quite successful on Instagram as it has attracted global interest in its products despite being localized in North America. Besides, Van initially appealed to teen skaters but presently focuses on showcasing their loyalty to teenage skating in a more engaging manner. In this case, Van is another brand which a large community of followers on Instagram and has, therefore, benefitted successfully over time.

Lego

Everyone has come into contact with Lego, a toy company established in 1932 and based in Billund, Denmark. With about five million followers on Instagram, Lego uses the toys to entertain adults using product plus for kids. If you are not following this brand, then you are missing a lot, especially if you are a fun-loving person. For instance, Lego posted a video on Instagram, imitating the Royal wedding in 2018 using toys. The video garnered more than 100,000 views over the first few weeks. Through the #RoyalWedding hashtag, Lego promoted its brand, reaching more individuals who joined the Lego Instagram community.

When mentioning about the success of Instagram towards the company, Lego uses the video to show the public about it is not all about the toys, but more. That is, the products they distribute can do more than just being for kids to play with and have fun. When they accompanied the video with the hashtag, it attracted more people to the video as the #RoyalWedding was trending worldwide at the time. Therefore, Instagram became a platform that promoted the success of Lego while building customer reputation and increasing popularity among people around the world. Marketers can, therefore, take some useful information that that when utilizing trending hashtags and relevant visuals, the chances are that you are likely to succeed on Instagram.

ESPN

Truth be told, not everyone likes following a page with constant news or sports with a similar unending form of information over and over again. Many like fun and sometimes remove the seriousness that accompanies a given post to make it engaging and for ease of enjoying the moment. However, many television and radio news channels struggle with this problem as they work to attract the general population to follow and acquire their services. Typical news or sports channel can manage to get between 500 to about 2,000 comments on their feeds. Unlike most of these channels, ESPN uses a unique social media presence, which has made the sports channel among the most loved and followed on Instagram.

ESPN uses the most engaging strategies, such as asking for online quizzes about favorite teams or related content, which readily triggers emotions of sports lovers. Such questions usually influence an individual to answer or make a decision about a particular aspect. In this case, people are likely to become more engaging with subjects, and henceforth would love having a similar interaction more often. Therefore, ESPN would garner more followers while increasing engagements over time. Consequently, it would lead to an increase of comments to up to 30,000 to 100,000+ thousands of any given feed on Instagram. This technique has enabled the channel to become one of the leading sports channels, more so in social media interactions.

Lorna Jane

Unlike most brands that use feeds on Instagram to engage, attract, and have a significant number of followers, Lorna Jane uses a unique form of becoming successful in social marketing. Lorna Jane is a brand in Brisbane, Australia, which primarily deals with the manufacturing and distribution of women activewear founded in 1990. The brand was founded and owned by Lorna Jane Clarkson and Bill Clarkson. There are multiple ways the company markets its products and gain popularity in Australia. On Instagram, however, the Lorna Jane uses an entirely new technique of marketing. Instead of posting products on their feeds, the company uses a person who displays an active lifestyle resulting from the products provided by Lorna Jane.

With nearly one million followers on Instagram, Lorna Jane photos on their feeds show how a young, active, sporty, and jovial woman is living a life impacted by the brand. In most cases, brands prefer uploading their own products on Instagram with an excellent frame accompanied by costs or other related components. However, Lorna Jane uses a person as a driving force to engage and showcase clothing and accessories with colorful, inspirational, and attractive products. This strategy, therefore, enables followers as well as other targeted potential clients to engage and have a taste of the lifestyle portrayed. As a result, Lorna Jane has become among the most successful brands on Instagram, especially in Australia.

Huda Kattan

Many people are familiar with Huda Kattan, who is widely known as a professional makeup artist in the United States. Born in Oklahoma City, Oklahoma, Huda Kattan is recognized across all social media platforms, including Instagram. Beginning as a blogger writing about her passion for beauty, she transformed her marketing strategies to Instagram, where she created a page of her brand. Today, Huda Kattan has nearly 40 million Instagram followers who primarily embrace, seek, and admire her work and distribution in the beauty and fashion industry.

When we talk about how Instagram impacts the success of a person, one of the best examples is that of Huda Kattan. She has grown from a blogger, talking about her passion for making women beautiful, to creating an online community with millions of people behind her celebrating her actions. Instagram is all about visual, beauty, and fashion. Therefore, when you wish to succeed, grow, and build yourself as a person, then Instagram provides an ample platform to display your work. It eventually makes it more interactive while taking over the interest of others, making you among those who prosper online.

Cameron Dallas

Being an internet personality is never far from Instagram and other social media platforms. That is, it may make you become one of the best successful individuals globally. Take an example of Cameron Dallas, an American internet personality born in 1994 in Whittier, California, United States. Cameron began at Vine and YouTube, making videos and posting them. Over time, he joined Instagram, creating a massive community of more than 21 million followers. His presence and work caught the attention of other prominent organizations, including Netflix, and was hired to host a show, Chasing Cameron.

Cameron Dallas began creating short videos and songs and posting on different social media and forums, which also included Instagram. Over time, his Instagram account began growing, with the number of followers continually increasing. Similarly, other accounts, including Vine and YouTube, as well as Facebook and Twitter, created a more significant community of fans. His posts on Instagram are charismatic, engaging, and touching; therefore, building the connection he has towards his followers. Thus, Cameron Dallas proves that not only does showing off personality gains you popularity, but it also can land you a significant fandom.

Selena Gomez

This is with no doubt that if you have been to Instagram, you have heard or caught a glimpse of Selena Gomez on one or more occasions. Selena Gomez became the most followed person on Instagram for three years consecutively until when Cristiano Ronaldo surpassed her. With the current follower of more than 157 million on Instagram, Selena Gomez is a widely recognized celebrity influencer using her status to encourage charitable causes. For instance, her Instagram feeds comprise of several posts, most of which accompanying initiatives against actions that go against human rights, for example, human trafficking.

Besides, she also posts about her personal photos, which readily enable her to engage with her fans, making her among the best social media influencers. On one occasion, when asked about her vast fan base, Selena Gomez stated that of is vital to remain in connection with your followers, especially when interacting with them. She also mentioned about the consistency and provision of raw self to them instead of using others to act on your behalf. As among the top 10 most-followed people on Instagram, Selena Gomez is quite successful in her career and social interaction online more so, on Instagram.

Cristiano Ronaldo

As mentioned, Cristiano Ronaldo is the most followed person on Instagram, with more than 183 million followers. The Juventus football club megastar and a five-time Ballon d'Or winner is listed third on the top paid Instagram Influencers with $750,000 per sponsored feed. Cristiano Ronaldo's Instagram followers are always kept interactive and engaging in several topics he posts. For instance, the Juventus soccer team player has a partnership with Nike, where he posts about the company's products. Similarly, Cristiano posts about his underwear brand marketing about the product as well as other sponsorship.

Other than marketing and showcasing about his career, Cristiano Ronaldo is passionate about posting about personal life while updating his followers about what happens in his life. More so, he displays his family, game, and training posts, which with no doubt, keeps his followers connected and always talking about him. Like Selena Gomez, Cristiano Ronaldo often posts and keeps his fans committed to sharing what they have about him. Therefore, he keeps his followers frequently interested in his posts, thus, building his fan base daily. He has identified as an individual who most successful on Instagram, especially in posting and sharing enjoyable and high content regularly.

Daily Dose

With more than 1.6 million Instagram followers, Daily Dose is a digital marketing enterprise offering daily motivational quotes. It is the first and the most extensive growing account featuring powerful messages which are in the form of encouragements and building blocks of daily activities of an individual. Daily Dose primarily channels these posts to those in the Fortune 500 industry. Established by Tim Karsliyev, Daily Dose is estimated to impact more than 200 million people globally. The founder stated that his main objective is to change and make a difference to people who seem to have lost hope or whose hopes have faced challenges.

On their feeds, Daily Dose uses memes and pictures as well as other visual formats to create encouragement quotes essential for different groups. As to promote people to engage in their posts, Daily Dose uses a simple but quite effective technique that readily relates to Instagram followers. The posts are usually quoted shareable, and followers can relate to their lives but with positive intentions, especially for those who feel down or abandoned. More so, you can readily adopt and implement these messages to your daily lives without negative consequences. Daily Dose, like most successful Instagram accounts, has shown significant efforts to build a substantial fan base from unique content in their feeds.

Apartment Therapy

Garnering more than 2.2 million followers since launching the account, Apartment Therapy has become another successful brand in offering online therapy through showcasing mind relaxing residences. Photos and pictures found on Instagram account feed show something unique and very creative. For instance, the last two pictures in the accounts friendlier environments with unique features. If you have ever come into contact with these pictures, then you are familiar with the cozy homes they found in their feeds and the surroundings, which are noise-free and green.

When Apartment Therapy began, many were unfamiliar with how they are to impact the lives of others with pictures. However, the same now can be seen with an ever-growing follower count, which significantly has enhanced the success of the business. Referred to as Apartment Therapy, the homes posted accompany an excellent environment for a comfortable home, especially for home lovers with limited access to such luxurious apartments.

Conclusion

Instagram is a social media service built around sharing photos and videos. Instagram advertising is a method of spending money to share sponsored content on Instagram to reach a larger, more targeted audience. While there are various reasons as to why businesses may decide to advertise, Instagram ads are often utilized to grow the brand's image, generate new leads, increase website traffic and convert current leads into sales.

Instagram being a visual platform, doesn't need text ads. You, therefore, need an image or sets of images, a video, or a GIF to reach out to your target audience via Instagram ads. The best part of it is that Instagram advertising works! Around March 2017, stats show that over 120 million Instagram users either visited a website, called, got directions, emailed, or direct messaged to inquire about businesses based on an Instagram advertisement. Instagram says 60% of users discover new products and services on the platform, and over 75% of them go ahead and take action after being inspired by the ad.

Just like other social media platforms, spending money on an advert will lead to increased exposure for your brand as well as the opportunity to control who can see your ad. So, if you are not using Instagram ads, you are honestly missing out!

Finally, if you found this book useful in any way, an honest review is always appreciated!

www.ingramcontent.com/pod-product-compliance
Lightning Source LLC
Chambersburg PA
CBHW031908200326
41597CB00012B/549